My Friend's
FOOTPRINTS IN THE SNOW

---------- ≠ ≠ ≠ ----------

David A. Sigafoos, Ph.D.

The characters in this book are actual persons. The story form was taken from the author's real life experiences.

My Friend's FOOTPRINTS IN THE SNOW

THE AUTHOR

Dr. Sigafoos is a master high school educator and a very well known athlete and corporate leader in the State of Colorado. His name has been attached to hundreds of articles in local and state newspapers.

Sports talent was natural for Dr. Sigafoos as a six year old baseball pitcher. In high school, he lettered four years making all-conference all four years and pitched successfully against all seniors in the Colorado All-Star game as a freshman. As a junior, he pitched in the State baseball tournament. Dr. Sigafoos refused an offer to play professional baseball.

Basketball was a success also. He received honors: all-conference, all-state, and Denver All-Metropolitan. He broke the Colorado State Tournament game scoring record as well as the Colorado State All-Star Game scoring record. He received 82 university scholarship offers from around the country. Dr. Sigafoos accepted a Division One NCAA scholarship to Colorado State University where he played in the NIT Basketball Tournament and the NCAA Basketball Tournament. As a senior, he received a career ending injury and went back to school to work on his M.Ed. in order to teach and coach in high school.

As a teacher in high school, Dr. Sigafoos installed the nation's first IBM PC computers at three high schools. Later, he installed a PC network that was the nation's first in a high school. He did contract work for IBM traveling all over the country becoming known for his PC software expertise. Later, he became employed full time by IBM Global Services. Dr. Sigafoos also taught computer at the college level.

A native of Colorado, Dr. Sigafoos lives in a Denver suburb with his wife Allegra Kay. Their daughter and husband have one child. When not speaking or writing, Dr. Sigafoos, a dedicated fly fisherman, can be found in the Colorado high country on a stream or lake using artificial flies that he created.

ACKNOWLEDGEMENT

Thanks to my wife, Allegra Kay (Ross) Sigafoos, who as my new wife, stuck with me in her prayers and her presence knowing that I would probably lose my hands and feet due to this tragic accident. She knew in her heart that God would deliver me from my snowy grave and physical devastation.

Also, much appreciation is given to my wife for her tireless hours editing this book. Also much appreciation is given to Blenda Sue Pruitt for her expertise in editing this book.

My Friend's
FOOTPRINTS IN THE SNOW

Table of Contents

BOOK I

A CHAMPION AT WORK

BOOK II

THE EXCITEMENT OF SNOWMOBILING

BOOK III

STAYING ALIVE AT ALL COST

BOOK IV

SAVED FROM CERTAIN DEATH

BOOK V

DISASTEROUS PAIN AND STRESS

x

CHAPTER 1

<u>Competition</u>

CHAPTER 1

"Twenty three strikeouts?" "Yes, twenty three strikeouts" I said. He asked another question, "These were all in one game?" "Yes," "one game," I replied. I came back; "You are reading the newspaper article on the game, why don't you believe it?"

My friend was grilling me on my baseball career as a young man. We were in a friendly argument trying to out do each other's athletic accomplishments. We were competitors. This was an activity that demonstrated this competitiveness. Even sitting on the sofa, we were competing with each other.

It was fun looking back over the past with my old teammate. It was especially interesting to play out the highlights of a life that took a real twist on top of a frozen mountain. Near tragedy occurred on this mountain. My friends and I nearly lost our lives because of this same competitiveness. On this mountain, I was buried in the snow for seven hours and lived to write about it.

Competition was my life. It started early in elementary school. I found quickly that during recess, I excelled in the many games and activities. The other kids would often pick me first to be on their team. I was always the tallest kid in class. By the time I reached sixth grade, I was five feet ten inches tall. I grew two inches every year through my senior year in high school. I especially enjoyed baseball, football, and basketball. These sports were fun and the teams on which I played won numerous games. The competition with other teams and winning became a large part of my life.

Baseball was always my favorite sport. I enjoyed being a pitcher. It was as if I was in control of the game. Every time I played, it was like putting a puzzle together. The competition when facing a batter was exhilarating!

One experience I remember well became one of my favorites. It happened during my freshman year in high school. There was a great senior athlete who was three years older. He had an exceptionally great high school career in football, basketball, and baseball and became one of the greatest and most powerful players to play in the State of Colorado. He was offered NCAA scholarships in all three sports. I was pitching a game as a freshman against this great player's team. This team, I was playing against, was in first place in our league because of this player.

We got to the last inning and surprisingly, we were ahead by one run. I made a mistake and let a batter hit a double with two outs. I had wanted to end the game there because this great player was coming up to bat. He was a tremendous hitter and always got good wood on the ball. He was three for three, all singles. Striking out was something that he rarely did.

My coach came out to talk to me. He told me that he would rather I would walk him and put him on first base then to give him a chance to get another single and tie the game. He had won many games in the last inning with his great hitting.

I told my coach that my concern was that if I put him on base; he would represent the winning run. If the next batter, who was also a good hitter, got an extra base hit the game would be over. I reminded my coach that I had played summer ball with this batter and I knew where to pitch to him. Of course, he knew all of this. He looked at me and sarcastically said, "This batter has been up three times and has hit three singles!" He shook his head and said that he was not sure that I knew where to pitch to him.

When a coach comes out to the mound to talk to a pitcher, the pitcher always says that he can get the next batter out, no matter what. Pitchers are rather dishonest. No pitcher wants to be taken out of a game especially when his team is in the lead. My coach looked at me with much doubt. I said that I was not tired and to give me a chance. He reminded me that if I was wrong, I was letting my whole team down. I tried to look tough, but letting my whole team down was not something I wanted to do. The home plate umpire came out to the mound to break up our conversation. I was glad he did.

As my coach walked off, I started thinking about this player. He had hit three singles off me! I was thinking that if he hit a hard single to a fielder, like he usually did, maybe we would hold the runner on third and from scoring. Then there would be a runner on first and third. If he hit a homerun, then I would walk off the field with a loss and probably would not be able to face my coach or my team. I thought for a minute that maybe I made a mistake. I looked at my coach walking into the dugout and thought, what in the world was I thinking! It is too late now to change my mind. Maybe I was getting tired and needed to be relieved by a fresh pitcher.

This batter was a terrific inside pitch hitter. Most of his hits were blue-darters down the third base line. Facing him this time, I knew that physically, I was tired and would not overpower him. I needed to face him and get him out mentally. I needed to out think him.

As my coach repositioned the infielders and outfielders to be ready for a hard hit to the left, I was able to clear my head. I walked around the mound, picked up the rosin bag, and thought to myself that this batter knows me well and I know him. I had pitched batting practice to him many times last summer in American Legion Baseball. I was a scrawny young man who was a rookie and did not play that much. In my mind, I thought that I was a pretty good pitcher. But, when I pitched to him, I was bombarded by line drives coming at me. I ducked many times when he hit a ball toward the mound. In one game, he hit a line drive right at a pitcher, hitting him in the head. The pitcher looked lifeless when an ambulance took him to the hospital. Even though this pitcher lived, every pitcher this player faced, remembered this. Facing him in the past, I never did figure out how to pitch to him.

I am sure that he was expecting all the pitches to be outside. Every pitcher in our league knew that he was a good inside pitch batter. All season long, he got most pitches outside and this is why he led the league with walks. Pitchers were afraid of him.

I studied him and saw that he had closed his stance so that he could reach the outside corner of the plate. I had not noticed this earlier when pitching to him. Since he was "crowding" the plate, I pitched a fastball inside to him trying to catch the corner. He fell back like he was thinking that I was trying to hit him giving me a dirty look. The umpire called a strike and the batter now looked at him with an unhappy look. Well, the first surprise worked. On the next pitch, I took a little off the fastball and pitched a changeup inside again and got lucky. He missed with a wicked swing for strike two. With his power, he was way out in front of the ball. I was amazed and so was my catcher that he didn't hit the ball out of the ballpark. Because of this pitch, my catcher came out to the mound and said that I pitched a great ball but what in the world was I was doing! He told me to play around with him since I had two strikes.

I knew that he was right. I had better be careful. I pitched the next three pitches way outside the plate. I hoped that he might swing at a bad pitch and hit a ground ball to one of our infielders. He was too smart to do this.

Now the count was two strikes and three balls. If I walked him, nothing would be lost and my coach and my team would be happy. My third baseman came over to me and told me to go ahead and walk him. I thought that maybe I was letting my team down by pitching to this batter. I was too much of a competitor to quit now. Besides, if I walked him, my coach was probably going to take me out of the game. He had our relief pitcher warming up in the pitchers cage.

In my mind, I was thinking that the batter was expecting that I would put everything I had into a fast ball and pitch an inside pitch again. I threw a slow sweeping curve on the outside edge of the plate. He let it go by for a called strike and the third out. I couldn't believe that I struck this guy out! We won! I don't think that anyone else could believe it either.

After taking the third strike, this player, who outweighed me by about 100 pounds started running out towards the mound and still had the bat in his hand. I panicked and froze where I stood on the mound! There was no escape. He ran a lot faster than I could.

His coach, who was coaching first base, also started running towards the mound. My coach started running towards me from the dugout. The two umpires were also converging on the pitching mound. The mound was about to be a meeting place for a bunch of people. I was hoping that everyone would get there before this player. This player was the first to get there. He came up to me and put out his hand to shake mine. He then said, "Congratulations, Dave, you pitched a great game!"

This has to be one of the most emotional experiences that I have ever had. This guy was huge and tough. I thought that I was dead! He was an all-state quarterback, all-state basketball player, and an all-state baseball catcher. And, I might add, an all-state great sportsman! Praise God!

CHAPTER 2

<u>Several Thousand People</u>

CHAPTER 2

My freshman year was so successful in baseball that I was invited to participate in the yearly Colorado North/South All Star Game at Bear's Stadium in Denver, Colorado. This stadium was renamed to Mile High Stadium that Denver Bronco great John Elway made famous. Remember the Mile High Salute?

I played for the South squad. Being a freshman, I was sure that I was on the bottom of the list to play ball that night. I was proud to be there but also scared to death because I was so young. Every player on both teams was mostly seniors and juniors. I was hoping that I would be a spectator and not a player. I had never played in front of thousands of people. Most of the pitchers in the bullpen were seniors, players that I had admired and watched as a lowly freshman. I had learned much from them.

As the game proceeded, the North squad was beating our South team by several runs. It was a one sided game. It got to the last inning and I was relieved that the game was about over. The game was out of reach for the South. It was just pride that was keeping the South in the game. There was a senior pitcher, a junior pitcher, and myself in the bullpen. I was relieved that the odds were in favor that I would not have to "embarrass myself."

The bottom of the batting order was due up, thank goodness for our team. Surely our pitcher would get them out in order. The North coach put in a pinch hitter. The pinch hitter hit a single on the first pitch right up the middle. This made me feel a little nervous.

The North coach put in another pinch hitter, a left hander. Our coach went to the mound and waved in our left-hand junior pitcher. This batter got another single.

Now there was a runner on first and second base and no outs. Now, of all things that we did not want, the top of the batting order was up with their best hitters with two runners on with no outs. Our coach came out to the mound and looked to the bullpen. There were two right hand pitchers warming up and I was one of them. He asked for the other right hand senior pitcher.

I was feeling pretty good that the pitching coach sent the other pitcher out. I had escaped the bullet again. This pitcher got the next two batters to ground out very quickly. No one in the stadium was happier than I was! Things were looking up for me because there was now two outs! It looked as if I would get out of this game without having to pitch.

The third batter in the starting order, drag bunted down the third base line and got on first, loading the bases. He was able to do this because he was a power hitter and our third baseman was playing him deep. I could feel blood rising into my face as the coach walked to the mound and asked for the ball. He waved me in. The North fans booed because they wanted the game over. They were ready to go home with the victory and did not want to sit there and wait for another pitcher to warm-up.

Being skinny as a rail standing about 6'4", I really did not want to go out to that pitching mound. When a pitcher goes to the mound, the many hundreds or thousands of people watch and measure him up to see if he is worthy. If he is a skinny 6'4" freshman, the noise can be rather disturbing. The bad mouth talk from the opposing dugout is bad enough yet alone the many opposing fans in the stadium. This might have been an honor to pitch in an all star game but so far it was a nightmare.

I walked in from the bullpen and looked at the several thousand people who were looking at me. The opposing fans and the opposing team in the dugout were jeering me. When I got to the mound, I could see that the pitching coach was concerned. He told me to not think about the crowd and just think about the batter that I was going to face. I knew he was right but it was hard to concentrate.

The worse thing happened. My first warm-up pitch went wild over the head of the catcher. This made the jeers louder then ever. The batter that was standing there studying and measuring me started laughing and pointed his finger at me. I could not get my other warm-up pitches over the plate. This pitching mound was for a professional team and was higher then I had ever pitched. In our league, we did not have raised pitching mounds. Also, I was so nervous that I could not get the ball down to the plate. All the pitches were high. The catcher came out to the mound and told me that he knew that I could do it. Just relax and pitch.

The terrifying thing was that this jeering batter that was pointing a finger at me was the fourth man in the order. These batters are put in the fourth position to clear the bases. The last time at bat, he cleaned the bases by hitting a double off the centerfield scoreboard. I was aware of him from the Denver Post newspaper. He had been clearing the bases all season and was the City of Denver batting champ. He was one of the State's best players. Of course, this is why he was in the all-star game.

The bases were loaded and here I was not able to find the plate. Normally, I was pretty sure of myself when I pitched. But now I felt like Daniel in the lion's den. The lions were all around me ready to pounce on me. I was thinking that the coach was either being nice getting me into the game or he was mad at me. I had pitched twice against his team in our league and we had won both games. These were the only two losses for his team. Maybe he was trying to get even. This was the team that had the state's best player on it that I was lucky to strike out. My thinking went to this great player. Now, he was the catcher to whom I was pitching.

I took a deep breath of air and picked up the rosin bag trying to relax. The nightmare question I was asking myself was what would happen if this batter hit a home run? He had done it many times before. Everyone including my own team would laugh me out of the stadium. Also, there were no more pitchers. Who would end the game? I prayed for a power failure and that the game would be called due to darkness.

The catcher asked for a fastball. I paused a moment and the thought came to me that if I threw over the catcher's head again, a runner would score. I cleared my mind and I threw the first pitch down the middle of the plate for a strike. This was stupid to do to the best batter in the state! I was surprised that he let it go. He was not expecting such a good pitch. I, as well as everyone in the stadium, was surprised that I got it over the plate.

The batter was not happy. He seemed a little embarrassed that he had let it go. He had probably not seen a pitch go down the middle of the plate for him all year. He dug his cleats into the dirt and gave me a look as if he was going to drill the next ball right through me. I threw a sweeping curve ball for another called strike. Due to my long arms and pitching side armed, I had a large sweeping curve. Players on my team had told me that when I threw this pitch, it looked as if it was coming from third base. Most batters were unsure what to do when a side arm pitched ball started behind them and swept over the plate. He was visually very mad at me. He probably had not had two called strikes in a row all year.

I knew that now he was going to have to swing at the next strike I threw and I had run out of surprises. With two strikes and no balls, a pitcher usually throws a couple of pitches outside the edge of the plate hoping that the batter will swing at a bad pitch.

I was still scared to death on that mound pitching in front of the largest crowd that I had ever seen. Because I had thrown two strikes, they were now fairly quiet. I knew that I was shaking all over with fear. I decided that I would challenge him and hopefully get out of there. The only surprise that I could think of was to send another down the middle of the plate. He knew in his mind that no intelligent pitcher would throw another down the middle. He would definitely not expect a good pitch.

I didn't like the look he was giving me. I knew that the crowd was just waiting for him to clear the bases. It was just a matter of time. It was strange how quiet the crowd was. They were in shock that a freshman had two strikes on this batter. I reared back and threw another fast ball down the middle of the plate. He took a big swing and missed. He was behind my pitch. I had actually surprised him. I think that he was expecting the curve ball again. It was like the old story when the mighty Casey struck out!

After three strike pitches, I walked to the dugout acting like I did this type of thing every day. The team and the fans did not know that I felt like fainting. My legs were like rubber. Thousands of people, friend and foe, were on their feet clapping and yelling for me, a freshman. They were probably just clapping because the game was about over.

As I entered the dugout, players and coaches alike shook my hand. They hadn't had much to be happy about that night. Our coach came to me and said, "The fans are yelling for you. Go up and take a bow!" I was embarrassed to do so. Of all things, I did not want to do was to go out again! As I went up out of the dugout to wave at the crowd, something happened that would remain in my mind for years to come. I took my hat off and stepped out from the dugout. I put my hand up to wave and turned around and glanced up at the crowd. I immediately focused on one face. It was my own high school coach. I did not even know that he was at the game. He was in the middle of thousands of fans and was also on his feet clapping. He gave me two "thumbs up." Wow, what a Rocky Mountain High! It was a good thing that no one said anything to me immediately after that because I was too emotional to talk.

This led to another three years pitching for my high school. At the end of my senior year, I had an offer to pitch professional ball. I declined. Other things had happened that were to change my life.

We went to state in baseball and also basketball. We won the state championship in basketball when I was a senior and I broke the state scoring record with the help of some great teammates. All-conference, all-Denver Metro, and all-state honors sent notice to colleges across the nation.

Playing in the Colorado All-Star Basketball Game in Pueblo, Colorado, was a great honor, especially after scoring 33 points and breaking the scoring record. All of these honors led to a basketball scholarship. My basketball coach received most of my scholarship offers. He told me that he had 82 scholarship offers in his file.

I also had scholarships for baseball but I decided that due to my size, basketball would be more of a future. By this time, after growing two inches a year, I was now 6'10" tall.

CHAPTER 3

<u>LA Sports Arena</u>

CHAPTER 3

College basketball led me to great cities all over the nation. At one juncture during my junior year, the Associated Press Poll rated us as the third top team in the nation. A great experience that year was when we played UCLA who was coached by the great John Wooden. We played the game at our school and we beat them by one point.

I was thrilled after the game when Coach Wooden shook my hand and told me that I played a good game. I appreciated this because I knew Coach Wooden. He had sat in my living room trying to recruit me to play for UCLA a few years earlier.

A month later, we went to Los Angeles to play UCLA again at the Los Angeles Basketball Classic Tournament at the Sports Arena. My uncle showed me a newspaper story where Coach Wooden was being interviewed the previous week. He said about me, "He has the softest shooting touch west of the Mississippi." That was one of the greatest honors that I had ever been given. I carried that basketball clipping with me for years after that in my wallet.

The game against UCLA at the Sports Arena was a back and forth game that was close just like the game at our place. When the game was over, we lost by one point. They evened up the score with us. The year that we played UCLA was the first year of many for Coach Wooden to win the NCAA Championship. We were pleased that we were the only team to win a game against powerful UCLA that year.

Basketball in college was a successful journey my four years there. Our coach knew what he was doing. In my college career, we played in the NCAA Tournament and also in the NIT tournament in New York City at Madison Square Garden.

I felt that I was on top of the basketball world until I injured my right ankle, damaging tendons and ligaments. This was the spring of my junior year while working out in the gym. The doctor told me that I might not be able to play again. He was concerned in that I had been hit in a game in Montana during the season and had injured tendons in my right knee. Now the right ankle was in question.

You don't tell a competitor that he might not be able to play. I worked harder then ever in rehabilitation. I was determined to strengthen my ankle and my knee and finish my senior year. I ended up losing about one third of the movement in the ankle. This was before the wondrous surgeries where this type of injury could be cured. I played an average senior year, but not one the scouts were looking for. Well, so much for the draft and professional basketball.

CHAPTER 4

<u>Perfect Challenge</u>

CHAPTER 4

My good friends Jack and Irv were ice fishing with me in the beautiful Rocky Mountains at the base of Colorado's highest peak, Mt. Elbert. We were fishing Twin Lakes for Mackinaw trout. God's beautiful creation made us feel close to heaven. God's Word tells us that heaven will be more beautiful then this. It is hard to imagine!

This wonder of God's creation was on our minds as we looked over the beautiful snow-capped mountains that surrounded us. We could see three mountains that were over 14,000 feet in elevation.

We were watching two men and a boy snowmobiling at the far end of the lake. I have never been a real strong racing enthusiast but this looked like fun. I was at 29 years of age and still had not received a ticket for speeding. Watching these "speeders," it looked like speeding was fun. They were probably going between 30 and 50 miles per hour and having a wonderful time.

The boy looked as if he was probably fifteen or sixteen years old. He kept trying to tease his dad into a race. They were having a ball, probably better then us since we had not caught a fish all day and it was cold.

Watching intently, Jack said, "We should get some snowmobiles and have some fun." Jack and I went to a snowmobile dealer in Denver the next week and looked at several models. These snowmobiles were expensive when you threw in the trailer, suit, gloves, boots, goggles, and helmet. I decided that this was a rich man's sport and I opted out. I needed to be totally sold if I was going to spend that much money. Being teachers, our salaries weren't that big to spend it on a whim.

A few weeks later, Jack called and asked if I could come to dinner. I was single and he was married to a woman who knew how to cook in a big way. I never passed up an opportunity like this. After a pheasant dinner, two birds that we shot during a hunting expedition in November, he asked me to come to the garage where he showed me a brand new snowmobile.

By the end of the week, several of our friends had tried out the snowmobile and found it exciting. The acceleration from 0 to 60 miles per hour was tremendous! It was great fun. I was hooked. Now I had to get one, maybe a little faster then this one. How about that, the competition is back!

Irv and another teacher friend, Bill, went out the next week and found two fast snowmobiles and bought them. I was still a little shy of spending the big bucks on a snowmobile because I had just bought a new SUV. When I realized that I was being left out on weekend excursions, I found a used snowmobile with a big engine. Not realizing it at the time, this used snowmobile had much more power then my two friends. The competition was back and I was in the lead. Racing and power was the new game. I was the one on top most of the time.

Snowmobiling gave me the same type of feeling that I felt when I stepped onto the mound to pitch. I can remember that every time I pitched, there was a feeling of the unknown and a drive for power to overcome a barrier. With baseball, I had a team behind me but I felt that I was in control of my destiny. The big difference with snowmobiling was that there was no team behind me to back me up if I made a mistake. Also, there was not a hoard of screaming fans watching me and waiting for me to make that mistake. But there was the feeling of the unknown and the drive to overcome a barrier that I couldn't see.

Being 6'10", I could lean and hang my weight out further then anyone else and therefore was able to take curves faster and sharper. I entered a couple of snowmobile races at Winter Park and Vail, but I just was not cut out to race. One problem was that I was inexperienced and not very good compared to the other racers.

To be successful, I needed to be just a little crazy and reckless. I could not worry about running into people or trees or driving off cliffs. I found that I had to sacrifice my machine to severe damage of which I could not afford. It just did not seem worth sacrificing my body to win at this sport. I figured that I might marry some day and I needed all my body parts to make a run at that new type of competition.

Over a period of three years, Jack, Irv, and I spent many hours and days in the beautiful wintertime zipping over the snowy mountains and valleys. I was never one that enjoyed the cold and snow. But on these machines, it was exhilarating. You could climb a mountain and when you got to the top, the beautiful snowy view was breathtaking. I could now understand the mountain climbers. They have a daunting task figuring out how to get to the top of the mountain. When they get there, there is a beautiful reward waiting there.

The snowmobile gave me something to look forward to with winter coming since my injury-ridden body was having trouble playing winter basketball. For fifteen years straight, I played basketball every winter. Not doing this was creating a void. Snowmobiling filled this void. I really looked forward to the winter. Also, I could snowmobile with my bad ankle and knee without stressing them.

Athletically, snowmobiling was a perfect challenge for me. I could compete not only with my friends but also with the terrain and the snow. Because of basketball, my coach never allowed me to go skiing because of a possible injury. My coach would tell us that we were involved in a team sport. Other players, the university, and the fans would be affected by a ski injury. Because of this, I had never skied or got involved in outdoor winter sports.

Snowmobiling was easy to do without all the lessons that skiing would require. If you can drive a car, you can drive a snowmobile.

CHAPTER 5

<u>Hall Valley</u>

CHAPTER 5

The weather forecast for tomorrow was for a clear, very cold day around 20 degrees in Denver. Jack, Irv, and I planned on taking a short Saturday trip to go snowmobiling. An extremely cold day in the mountains did not bother us because we had snowmobile suits and boots that were made for the cold.

We did not feel comfortable venturing out in a snowstorm because pulling a snowmobile trailer on icy roads was putting our lives in jeopardy. But the next day was supposed to be clear and beautiful.

Irv had a new four wheel drive pickup to try out. We decided to go into the Rocky Mountains above Denver to see if this truck was as powerful as advertised with its 400 cubic inch engine. Last night, a snowstorm hit the Rocky Mountains and the weekend ski report was for clear, cold weather, and wonderful deep, powder skiing. We planned on finding this deep powder snow for good snowmobiling. Just like the skiers, we liked the powder snow flying around us.

I was surprised when I saw a brand new snowmobile in the back of the new pickup. Irv had bought a hot new snowmobile that was a different make than ours. It was supposed to be lightning fast. I had read about this machine in snowmobiling magazines. It had beaten just about all makes of snowmobiles in speed trials.

Irv's old machine was not as powerful as Jack's and mine. Irv was always last getting up the mountain and getting down the mountain. He was now making a statement. Overall, Irv was probably a bigger competitor than Jack and I. We had seen this on fishing trips. He would always run and beat us to the best fishing hole in the river and get his line in the water first. For sure, the competition of racing was back and I was not sure that I was going to appreciate being in second or third place when racing.

It was about twenty degrees when we left Denver about eight o'clock in the morning. We knew that in the mountains, it would be ten to twenty degrees colder then Denver. Denver was a mile above sea level and we were going up another mile or more to go snowmobiling. We were probably facing at least zero degrees at that altitude during the morning hours. We knew that this was a temperature that you could get frostbite if you didn't dress right.

We drove into the mountains to the town of Grant about 60 miles West of Denver. The cold mountain air went straight through us without our suits on. We could tell that it was much colder then it had been in Denver. We went into a small store at Grant and purchased packages of small doughnuts and soft drinks because we had not taken time to eat breakfast. This mistake was to become one of our worst enemies before this trip was through.

As we ate our snack, we drove to the turnoff that went to Hall Valley at the foot of Kenosha Pass, about three miles from Grant. We proceeded on a snow packed dirt road towards Hall Valley about two miles. Since it had snowed the day before, there was about five inches of new snow on the road. It had previously been snowplowed. There were two to three feet of snow along the edges of the road. We got to the end where the snowplow had plowed. At this point, there was too much snow for the four-wheel drive pickup to attempt to go further.

Because we were pulling a double snowmobile trailer, we had to make sure that we could get turned around and headed out in case of new snow coming in. You cannot depend on weather forecasts in the Rocky Mountains. The weather can change very quickly. You always need to be prepared for the worst to happen.

After we unloaded our three snowmobiles, we shed our sweaters and put on our snowmobile suits. The snowmobile suits seemed heavy enough without sweaters since the sunshine was getting warm. Heavy sweaters would make us perspire too much and we did not want to be damp in this cold. Besides, we were only to go for a couple of hours. It was sunny and hopefully it would warm up by noon. Too many clothes would hamper the fun.

Today was not a serious snowmobile day. We just wanted to try out the new pickup and also the new snowmobile. It would not be wise to venture off too far since we had not eaten. Maybe we would just run our snowmobiles up the flat valley for a while and then head home. Since this was the weekend, we had promised our wives that we would tend to some unfinished chores. By going snowmobiling, we already were treading on thin ice with our wives.

It had warmed to around 20 degrees. Irv decided that with the exercise that he was doing, he did not need his snowmobile suit so he went to the pickup and put on a light waterproof jumpsuit. I was chilled with the slight breeze blowing. I told him that I needed more than that since I was skinny and the cold bothered me. Irv was a little overweight; he had the insulation that I did not have.

Snowmobiling is a very physical sport. You need to constantly shift your weight back and forth to compensate for the uneven terrain as well as turning. You use much energy when you get stuck when you have to lift and push the machine around. You work up a sweat real fast and a heavy suit gets soaked with perspiration after a period of time. This causes a damp chill. With the cold, you do not want to have wet clothing inside the suit.

We decided that since it was such a beautiful day, we would go up the old mine road which went to the pass and then turn back. Whenever we would look at a road going up, it was hard not to investigate it. We guided our snowmobiles up the trail and toward Webster Pass. This pass goes over the Continental

Divide that drops into Montezuma, Dillon, and Breckenridge on the other side. Dillon is in the middle of ski country. On the Dillon side, the watershed goes to the West Coast. On the side we were on, the watershed goes towards the East Coast and the Mississippi River.

Being in front of us, Irv took off with a blast of power with powder snow flying all around. He did have an extremely fast machine. We started up the old gold mine road that was blasted through the rock for wagons. We went up the trail a short distance and Irv got stuck. In fact, he was hopelessly stuck in two to three feet of powder snow. We had only been going up the road for two minutes and he was stuck.

We kidded him as we watched him lift his machine out of the snow and back on the trail. Of course, we would not help him. He was too independent. Also, we were always in a type of competition to see who could get somewhere first.

He had quite a time getting up on top of the snow and running again. The narrow track machine was not very good in the deep powder. The machine was fast but if Irv slowed down, it would sink into the deep snow because of that narrow track. When it did get up on top of the snow, it would really fly. Irv was really hurt by his machine not working very well. I think that his idea was to lose both of us in his tracks and it just didn't happen. We tried to console him by telling him that his machine would work better on the flat areas that we most often played around in.

We sat for a while deciding what to do. Irv's machine was having trouble and maybe we should just go back and continue in the flat valley. But, there is something drawing you when you see a mine road going towards a pass and it is a perfect day. What does the pass look like? Where does it actually go? There was a type of competitive spirit that hit us. We had to climb this mountain.

We decided that I would take the lead for now to break trail going up the mountain. I had a powerful wide track machine that seemed to stay on top of the snow as long as I kept moving, even slowly. As long as Irv kept on the trail that I was breaking, he was able to keep up. We were not worried about going too far because it was super fast coming down. We figured to go up about an hour and then turn back and trailer the machines.

Irv got stuck several times when his machine would stray off the broken trail that Jack and I were breaking. Occasionally, we would stop and walk back to help him get back on the trail. This was tough because the powder was so deep. Each step was difficult to take. You would sink up to your crouch. We would cringe when we would see him getting stuck because it was so hard to go back to help him.

We investigated many areas going toward timberline. Everywhere the trees would break into a clearing, we would go. These areas we were going up were probably old mine roads. We were not sure which road took us up to the top because it was difficult to see due to the deep snow. In fact, we did not know at times if we were really on a road.

Several times we investigated up toward slopes that had been cleared by avalanches. You could tell the avalanche areas by the trees lining the outside area. On the inside there would be a swath of virtually no trees or vegetation. We were always very cautious about places like this especially on a day after a good snowstorm. We never would venture out into a cleared out area. With the noise and vibration of our machines echoing off the mountains, an avalanche could break off without notice and be on top of us before we knew it. You can't escape a fast moving avalanche even on a fast snowmobile.

Finally we got to timberline, about eight miles from the pickup. There were miles and miles of rolling hills and mountains. We had a great time exploring the area for several hours. The day was so beautiful that we had lost track of time. The powder snow was so beautiful. It was like a dream. The hour turned into several hours. Our short trip was going to turn into a nightmare with our wives. I was sure that they were going to be upset!

All three machines could go 65 to 85 miles per hour. A lot of ground can he covered in a short amount of time when you are moving fast. We finally got on top of what we thought was Webster Pass. Everywhere there was snow. It was difficult to tell how much. Snow was measured in yards up there not inches. We thought that this was the pass because it had looked as if rocks underneath the snow had been moved or blasted to make a possible road. The beauty was unbelievable! You could see mountain ranges all around us.

It was about 3:30 p.m. We decided that it was getting late and that we should start heading back. Our wives would be wondering what in the world we were doing since we had promised a short trip. As we started down, the sun began going behind the mountain. With a trail broken, it would he a quick trip down to the pickup. Our experience with all the trips that we had made in the past made us know that the trip down the mountain was fast and easy since the trail had been broken. Going downhill was always extremely fast compared to going up. Going up was slow because we were constantly breaking the trail and also trying to figure out the best route to go.

We all had headlights and taillights so we were not worried about darkness. There were several times that we had gone snowmobiling at night. In a familiar area, this is wonderful to do with a full moon.
We were way above timberline, probably fifteen miles from the pickup. We figured that we would be back to the pickup in 30-40 minutes.

As we got part of the way down the hill, I thought that it would be wise to change my spark plugs since they had been fouling. My machine had been running erratically for the last few miles and smoke was coming out of the exhaust. Maybe I got a little too much oil in the gasoline—these were 2-cycle engines that required a gas/oil mix. Going down the mountain, I did not want to be last, of course.

As I changed the plugs, Jack and Irv opened cans of soft drinks. It was interesting popping the cans open. It made an echoing sound seemingly for a long distance. We joked that the popping sound might start an avalanche.

This country and the view were so magnificent! We sat and talked about this wonderful, clear day and the beauty of God's snowy creation. We also talked about how our wives would react when we got home. We had stayed all day instead of two hours.

We had not thought about how hungry we were getting since we were having so much fun. We sat there and the topic of hunger came up. All we had eaten were a fifty-cent package of small doughnuts and two cans of soda each. This was all for the whole day! We should not have skipped eating a meal.

Now we were going to move down the hill in a hurry to get to a restaurant to eat at Grant. Our biggest worry? Hopefully the restaurant would still be open.

CHAPTER 6

<u>Sliding off the Trail</u>

CHAPTER 6

What a wonderful day it had been. To see God's creation in its white snowy cloak was beyond description. The totally deep, blue sky and the glittering snow were something to behold. All of this beauty was surrounding us no matter what direction you looked. Who would have thought that it was something that would change my life drastically? I guess the old cliché, "the calm before the storm," was true in my case.

As I started down the mountain, I noticed a considerable difference in my snowmobile. With the change of the spark plugs, it ran much better. Jack and Irv told me to take the lead in case my snowmobile faltered. As I lead us down about 40-50 miles per hour, I could barely see trees of the timberline ahead. It was now getting towards 4:00

p.m. It was getting harder to see ahead due to the shadow of darkness with the sun going further behind the mountain. I could see the dark outline of the trees against the white background of the snow.

At timberline, I slowed down. There was a very sharp turn around a rocky area where the road led into the trees. As I turned slowly around the corner, the left ski of my snowmobile bounced off a rock or a ridge of ice that threw my snowmobile to the right down a sharp embankment.

It happened so quickly that I didn't have time to react about getting my weight over to the left. My snowmobile started sliding off the trail and I couldn't control it. If I could have leaned my body to the left, I maybe could have kept control and kept on the trail. I could barely hold on as I slid sideways down the steep embankment. Finally, I made it onto a flat area between rock and tree lined sides. I was lucky to stay with the snowmobile. It could have rolled over me if I had let go.

Once you go down an embankment like this, you must keep your snowmobile moving to keep up on top of the snow. The deep drifts of snow in a small valley such as this could be terribly hard to get out.

Hopefully, if I could keep going, I might find a way to circle around and get back up on the trail.

The small valley that I had slid into was going down hill faster then the trail that I had been on. This was the main valley down the hill. I was concerned because there had to be a stream flowing underneath all the snow.

I needed to continue parallel to the upper trail and hope that I could get back to it. If this kept going down hill, I would have to stop and turn my snowmobile around in order to return because of cliffs. Stopping in deep snow like this was really not an option because of the difficulty getting back up on top. I was barely able to keep the snowmobile on top of the deep snow because I had to go so slow.

Keeping my balance, I noticed that there was a small opening ahead through the trees. I was concerned because when coming up, I could remember a steep cliff on this side of the trail with a small stream of water cascading down the rocks.

I thought that I would head toward this opening going slowly and cautiously just in case it dropped down out of sight. If I was lucky, it might lead me around a corner and up to the main trail. If it didn't, I would have to stop and physically turn my snowmobile around and get back to the trail the way I came in.

When I got about fifty yards from the trees, it looked like a dead end. There were trees on all three sides and the snow was extremely deep. I did not even consider going through the trees. There is usually a lot of down timber around trees. With the powder snow being so deep, it would be impossible to drive a snowmobile through. It would normally be just about impossible to even consider walking through an area like this without snowshoes.

I needed to turn around as quickly as possible and double back to our main trail and meet my friends. As I stopped to make the turn, I noticed Jack right behind me about fifty feet. Irv was about thirty feet behind him. There was not enough room in this narrow valley to keep moving and turn around. I straightened my snowmobile and continued going straight to the trees ahead. Maybe a miracle hole through the trees would be there.

When snowmobiling down a hill, we usually go single file following the trail made by our machines coming up the hill. Since I was in the lead, they followed me thinking that I had found a short cut.

Since Jack was so close, I glanced ahead and noticed that the opening was getting narrower. It looked like a long, narrow, tree-lined streambed, so I continued to approach cautiously. We definitely did not want to follow a streambed. The ice and snow would be too unstable.

I tried the best I could to wave him back. This was difficult because I needed both hands on the snowmobile to steer it correctly and to keep it on top of the snow. Yelling was impossible because of the noise of the snowmobile engines and also we could not hear each other very well because of our helmets and ear coverings.

I had tried to wave both of them back after I slid into the canyon. I was too far in front and it was getting too dark for them to see my hand. I was also too busy wrestling my snowmobile to keep it on top of the snow. Now they both could see that we in a questionable area with tremendously deep powder snow. They slowed their snowmobiles down and tried to keep about twenty to thirty yards spacing between us.

It is difficult to get a snowmobile up on top of deep powder snow and keep it there when moving that slowly. Finally, I put my hand up and moved it in circles to show them that it was a dead end and they needed to turn around. The canyon was too narrow to make a turn and it looked like there was no means of escape. This definitely was a box canyon with only one way out, the way we came in.

We were going to have to lift our snowmobiles around in the deep powder and try to power them back up on the snow. If we could do this, we could then proceed out of this canyon. I got off my snowmobile and little by little turned it. At this extreme altitude, around 11,000 feet above sea level, I had no oxygen to get my muscles going. We were in need of nourishment. Not eating breakfast, lunch, or dinner was taking its toll. I was one of those people who could not skip breakfast or I would get sick. I felt a weak sickness come upon me as if I had skipped breakfast.

I finally got my snowmobile turned around and sat on the seat to rest. I was not feeling very well. I glanced at Jack and Irv to see if they were having any success getting their snowmobiles turned around. Snowmobiles weigh about five hundred pounds. It is normally a hard job to lift them around in shallow snow. This was a gruesome task in this deep powder.

There had to be three to four feet of powder in this valley. I had never seen anything like this.

Jack was having trouble getting his snowmobile turned around. Athletically, he was very strong. But he was fighting a 500-pound snowmobile that outweighed him by 350 pounds. Also, he was 5'8" tall and his short legs were having trouble moving in the deep snow. I tried to walk to his snowmobile to help him but the snow was so thick, I sank in to my crotch. After struggling a bit, I ended up crawling through the snow to help him out. I needed snowshoes.

CHAPTER 7

<u>Blanket Sheet of Ice</u>

CHAPTER 7

When I got to his snowmobile, I laid there a moment trying to get oxygen into my lungs. We were both lying in the snow trying to get our wind. It was hard not to laugh but laughter broke out. We joked about our weakness and then got to work again.

Even when I got my breathing back, I was terribly weak from lack of food. I am sure that Jack felt the same way. Crawling through this snow was just about impossible. My mind kept thinking about our snowshoes that were hanging in Jack's garage at home. It is too bad that we could not have tied them onto the snowmobiles. But, they would have been in the way, as many times we had to stop and get our machines back on top of the snow.

Irv, who was a big and powerfully strong man, was laughing at us. He had already turned his snowmobile around and was ready to move out. He was lying back on the seat, enjoying watching us huffing and puffing trying to get Jack's snowmobile turned around. With the strength Irv had, he probably lifted his snowmobile around with one hand. Now, he had about thirty yards to go to get out of the canyon and up on the trail.

As we were struggling to turn Jack's snowmobile around, we heard a loud crack. Jack's snowmobile and I immediately sank into a two to three foot deep pool of water! I was standing in freezing cold water up to my crotch. I could feel the icy water running into my boots.

I tried to scramble out of the water but the sides were steep and slippery with ice. When I finally rolled my body out and on top of the snow, the water on the outside of my boots and legs began freezing immediately. My arms and hands also got wet from struggling to get out of the water.

I had never been in such a cold situation where water froze almost immediately on contact. My boots were full of freezing water. My snowmobile suit was fairly waterproof but I could feel water coming in around the seams. It was a good suit to repel snow but it was not made to swim in. I knew that my legs and feet were in trouble in this subzero temperature.

Lying on the bank, I tried to take my boots off to get the water out. I needed to wring my socks out. My boots had a frozen covering that made it impossible to get them unfastened with my numb, cold hands. Jack came over and tried to help me get them off. We decided that we would do this later when we got back up on the trail. We needed to get out as soon as possible and get warm at the pickup. The more time we spent trying to get my feet warm was a gamble in this cold.

Since I was lying on the bank, I lifted both of my legs up to let the water run out of my boots. This was a mistake because water just ran down my legs to my waist. This just soaked the insulation in my suit more then it was before.

My hands were the biggest problem right now because they were instantly numb. I needed them to get out of this predicament.

We determined that this pool must have had a very thin covering of ice and there was a large snow. The ice would have hovered around the freezing mark while the temperature outside and above the snow was sub-zero degrees. The ice never got thick so the strength was not there. Also, there was moving water in the stream below the ice. It did not take much weight to break through.

By now it was getting very dark and the temperature had fallen well below the zero mark. The weather forecasters had predicted subzero temperatures all through the mountains for the next several days. This was not uncommon for a January in Colorado. Looking how fast the water froze on me, we determined that the temperature was between –15 to –20 degrees.

It was hard for me to walk because of the blanket sheet of ice that covered my pants and boots. The three of us knew the serious consequences that I was in with both legs soaked in icy water and the temperature well below zero. This gave Jack and Irv a burst of new energy. Something had to be done immediately or there were consequences on the way that we could not face.

When the ice cracked, Jack jumped back and luckily just caught the side of the pool. He splashed some water on him. His legs were damp but not soaking wet. We now could see that Jack's snowmobile had been on top of a pool of water. The stream that we were following had deep pools or possibly a beaver dam! We figured that it was pools since we did not normally see beavers up at timberline. They usually like Aspen trees to make their dams. Aspen trees are usually a thousand feet or so below timberline.

As I was scrambling out of the water, Jack's snowmobile sank further into the pool. It was now totally submerged except for the top of the windshield. As we looked at his snowmobile, we knew that we would not be able to get it out. We would need a winch or come-along type of tool to lift 500 pounds out of a hole of water. I could barely get myself out of the deep hole. How could we lift a 500-pound snowmobile? If we could get it out, the snowmobile would have to be towed because the engine was totally immersed in the water. We were having trouble powering a snowmobile on top of the snow. We could not even consider towing it out.

Yet, we did not want to leave it because the creek would freeze over and we would not be able to get it out until spring when the snow and ice thawed. This was a two thousand-dollar investment literally going down the drain.

Because of the dollar investment, we began to rethink how to get this snowmobile out of the pool. I had a towrope in my snowmobile. I thought that we could pull his snowmobile out of the canyon with my snowmobile. If I could go back into the water and tie on the rope, maybe Jack could drive my snowmobile and pull it out. It would take a lot of effort and pushing to get the snowmobile up to be towed. Could we get enough traction?

Maybe if Irv could help push Jack's snowmobile along with me, we could get it out of the water and top of the snow. I was already soaked so I thought it was worth a try. Jack asked me if I was crazy because he felt that it would be impossible to pull the snowmobile out of the water hole. After Irv looked at the problem, he agreed. Yes, I was crazy! We were taking too long to figure all these things out. We needed to get going and Jack could ride double with me back to the truck.

Another serious problem happened that we were not expecting. As we were talking things over to see what to do next, the pool that Jack's snowmobile was in opened up completely across the narrow canyon. My snowmobile could not get by this wide deep pool and I could not go the other way because of the box canyon of trees and rocks.

After quick, serious deliberating, we decided that these two snowmobiles would not help us get out. We needed an action plan to get out and get out immediately because I was frozen.

Jack and Irv discussed our dilema and decided that I could ride double with him and get out as soon as possible. I needed to get the heater on in the pickup and save my legs. In my mind I thought going out on Irv's snowmobile might be impossible because of Irv's narrow track machine. Adding another 200 pounds to the top of his machine would really make it sink into the snow.

My hands and feet were frozen terribly bad. We knew that I had to be suffering from frostbite. We understood frostbite and were always being careful to keep our skin from being exposed to the cold. Frostbite can be terribly dangerous, even causing people to lose limbs. If Irv could get me to the pickup and get the heater working, he could get his heavy snowmobile suit on and come back for Jack. Irv was fighting the cold with his light suit.

To go eight miles to the pickup and back would take time but Jack had a heavy suit and he felt that he would make it. Maybe tomorrow we could come back with picks and axes and get his snowmobile out of the ice.

Thank God that we spaced our snowmobiles out as we went into the canyon. Irv's snowmobile was our only hope of getting out and it was close to the entrance to the canyon. The thirty yards to get out would be easy if we could get the snowmobile up on the snow.

In the back of our minds, we knew we were facing difficulties with Irv's machine. He had gotten stuck so many times coming up. We knew that it would be difficult going all the miles to the pickup and back. Would he be able to make it?

We crawled to his snowmobile to help him get it out of the powder. We laid there for a couple of minutes trying to get some oxygen into our lungs and maybe get some strength back. We both helped to get the snowmobile up on top of the snow and moving. With all three of us not eating all day, we had no strength to work at that 11,000-foot altitude. We were so happy to hear the sound of the engine and see Irv's snowmobile get on top of the snow and head out of the canyon.

Since my socks and boots had been saturated with icy water, my legs and feet were freezing and were very numb. I was shaking uncontrollably. All I could think of was the heater in the warm pickup. Jack told me to crawl as fast as possible to the canyon opening and ride double with Irv and get to the pickup. He said that he would try to start walking out if that was possible and he would meet Irv on the trail on his return trip.

CHAPTER 8

<u>Fatal Mistakes</u>

CHAPTER 8

Irv stopped and turned his snowmobile off when he got to the mouth of the canyon. We had talked it over and he was going to try to go up the hill and get on the main trail. The plan was that I would crawl up to the trail and then we would go together. I told Jack that he must feel sorry for me being frozen and was going to try to give me a ride up the hill. I really knew his snowmobile would not allow that. I was so cold that I would go for anything that would get me out of there.

Jack told me that he thought that Irv was probably stuck again in powder. Since Irv had been having a struggle all day getting stuck in the snow, it probably happened again.

It was getting dark and we could barely see him against the white background. I yelled at him asking him why he stopped. He yelled back and said that we had a serious problem.

It took a lot of crawling to get to Irv's snowmobile, about 30 yards to where he had stopped. We had no energy and needed oxygen. My confused mind was telling me to hurry up and get warmed up.

When we got to the mouth of the canyon where Irv had stopped, we saw another pool of water had opened where we had crossed down into the valley. Irv was trying to guide his snowmobile around the pool of water. He had tried to move around the pool on the right by putting his right ski against the wall of the canyon. He tried to squeeze by the side of the pool. His snowmobile slid into the water and the left ski jammed between some rocks. He turned off the engine and jumped to the dry side so he would not get wet.

The ski was under about a foot of water. Irv was lucky that he had not fallen into the pool or he would have been wet and frozen like me. One of us was enough to go through this pain.

After tugging and pulling, we decided that one of us needed to get into the water and reach down and pull the ski free or else it might break off. A break would end all hope!

I volunteered since my legs were numb and frozen from my toes to my thighs. What would a little more water hurt when you are already numb? My boots were heavy with ice and I am sure I would not make the feeling worse in my legs and feet if I got wet.

Before Jack and I started out towards Irv, I tried again to drain some of the water out of my boots. None came out! It was frozen! I unzipped my suit and tried to reach down my pant leg to feel my socks. My pants were frozen to my skin. I could not push my hand down to my knees. I figured if I pushed it, I would damage my frostbitten skin.

I tried to get my boots off again. My hands were so numb that I could not feel or see anything in the dark. Both boots were solid ice. This made it impossible to even consider getting them off. This is where reality hit me between my eyes. I was going to lose my legs! I was going to graduate from being 6'10" to being 3'10" in height.

We had been so busy trying to get out of the canyon; I had not tried again to wring the water out my socks. We were expecting to start out any minute but things kept happening. The temperature had to be around -20 degrees by now with the clear sky. My mind was telling me that I could not take any more of this extreme cold without warming up somewhere. Something, anything had to change!

Without saying anything, all three of us were aware of the seriousness of the problem that I was in. Jack and Irv were also extremely cold but they did not say anything because they were worried for me. I could sense their concern. We were very competitive but when it came to supporting each other, there was competition to see who could help the most.

These guys were the best. When a person is in need like I was there is nothing more important and nothing more comforting then to have people praying to our Lord and Savior for His help. Jack, Irv, and I were hunting, fishing, and snowmobiling partners but the most important thing is that we were Christian prayer partners. All three of us had accepted Jesus and knew of his wondrous power. Whatever was happening on this mountain, we felt that God was in control.

I needed more flexibility in my knees to lift Irv's machine out of the water. I broke the ice off the outside of my pant legs with my fists. This hurt my hands terribly bad because they were so cold and frozen. My fingers felt like pins and needles when I tried to use them. Terrible pain was ever present and it was taking over my entire being.

Now it was time to get wet again. I would have to reach down into the water with my hands and grab onto the ski and try to shake it loose. I took my snowmobile gloves off and laid them on the snow so that they would not get any wetter. I jumped into the water and reached down with my numb bare hands and grabbed the ski. It was hard to feel anything because my hands were so numb. Also, the darkness did not help as far as being able to see into the water. As I pulled the ski, I shook it back and forth sideways and it came loose.

I dried my hands the best I could under my armpits and put my snowmobile gloves back on. My gloves were nylon and leather but the water came into them from the top when I previously scrambled out of the water hole. The wet insulation inside my gloves was stiff because it had frozen.

My hands now felt as numb as my feet. My legs from my thighs down were numb. I could not feel anything. I was cold and shaking uncontrollably. I had to get warm. My confused mind was screaming for warmth. Something had to work!

I could not wait to hear the sound of the motor of that new snowmobile. All I could think of was getting to that warm pickup. What I was worrying about now was how long it would take for the pickup heater to get warm when we got down the hill. I was starting to panic. Thinking warm was the only thing keeping me going.

We had been talking how lucky we were that Irv's snowmobile was the one that was left. It was new and the likelihood of mechanical problems would be little. My snowmobile had been giving me problems earlier and we knew that Irv's snowmobile might be better then that to go the 16 mile round trip. The only question was the narrow track. We thought that God probably had a reason for having Irv buy this snowmobile. He knew that we would need a good snowmobile to get us out.

Irv pulled the starter rope. Then, of all things, the most heart-wrenching thing that could possibly go wrong happened. The starter rope broke! A brand new snowmobile and the starter rope broke! I was devastated beyond explanation. I needed warmth, now. It was like all hope had vanished. We had been trying so hard to get out of this predicament and everything we were trying failed.

I was so extremely cold with shakes beyond my control. How could I escape this terrible, painful ordeal that I had gotten myself into? My thinking was getting muddled, probably because of the likelihood of hypothermia setting in. As cold as I was, I should have developed a very fatalistic attitude. I knew that hope was escaping us but I think that my brain was thinking so slowly that it didn't cross my mind that we were in a possible deadly predicament.

We did not know what happened with the rope because it was so dark. Irv was dressed in his light jumpsuit and was probably suffering as much or more then anyone. He did not have much feeling in his hands. Maybe, he could not control his extreme strength and he pulled the rope beyond the end where it snapped. Or, there might have been a mechanical problem that made the rope weak. I tried to lighten up the problem by saying that maybe Irv had overlooked the factory recall on the starter mechanism. We all tried to laugh but it did not work.

I can still remember how discouraging it was seeing Irv standing there with a starter rope in his hand. The three of us just stood there in silence for a moment in disbelief.

By this time, it was getting too dark to see. We had planned to go snowmobiling for a couple of hours to try out the new pickup and the new snowmobile. When we left Denver, I had taken my snowmobile off my double trailer not giving thought that our emergency kit was in the back of my wife's snowmobile. It did not cross my mind since we were going up for just the two hours. We tried not to vocally tell each other that this could be a fatal mistake. We could see it in each other's eyes.

One important thing I remembered was the attitude of Christian brothers. None of us showed blame towards each other. We should not have started up the road to the pass since we were just going for a couple of hours. I had driven off the road and had gotten us into this mess. Irv had broken the starter rope. We had not eaten. Our first aid kit was somewhere else. We were not dressed properly for severe weather. Every one of these things was a rookie mistake.

Never was there a complaint towards each other. This was how true competitors functioned. This was the best of competitive sportsmanship. Now the competition turned to a game of survival.

Even with all these crazy things that happened, many people would naturally accuse someone of making these fatal mistakes. Christ was in us. He took the blame on himself and set us free.

CHAPTER 9

<u>Situation was Grave</u>

CHAPTER 9

We had no flashlight or matches. None of us were smokers, therefore, no matches or lighter. We joked later that if you go snowmobiling, always bring a smoker with you. Yes, we were feeling a little stupid about now. Sixteen years of combined college education between us did not help our lack of common sense.

Our only hope was to get the only working snowmobile running or we would be in deadly trouble. Twenty degrees below zero, clear and dark with no moon, eight miles from the warmth of the pickup, terribly hungry and weak, three to four feet of powder snow to fight, no snowshoes, and no matches. One of us had a light jumpsuit and was freezing and the other had frozen legs, feet, and hands. What could be worse outside of an avalanche coming down on top of us? At this point, I really did not care.

We decided that one of us should try walking out while the other two tried to get the rope starter fixed. All three of us knew that walking out without snowshoes was impossible. This just made the hopeless feeling worse. The mechanism on the side of the engine had to be dismantled and the rope put back into the spring mechanism.

We decided that Irv probably should not be the one to walk out. He admitted that there was no way that he could possibly walk through that snow due to his 250 pounds of weight. Just like us, he was also having a terrible time moving in the deep powder. There was no way that he could possibly make it, even to the top of the hill to the trail.

Irv was the best mechanic between us. He probably was the best person to understand how to repair his snowmobile. Jack and Irv decided that it shouldn't be me to walk out because I had frozen feet and legs and was also too heavy to walk in the snow. I could not feel anything when I walked. They were concerned that I could injure myself further if I tried to walk.

Jack weighed somewhere between 160-165 pounds with his snowmobile suit and gloves on. He was having a terrible time trying to walk in the snow but we felt that with his lighter weight he had the best chance to make it out. He was also in terrific shape physically.

It was shortly after 6:00 p.m. when he started walking out or I might say crawling up the hill in the darkness. As I started moving back down toward my snowmobile to get tools for the repair, I could just barely make out the sound of Jack's hard breathing as he inched up the hill. I couldn't see him. I was really discouraged because if he went this speed for eight miles, it would take several days to get out.

I needed warmth now. I was desperate. I could not stand this any longer. The constant shakes were getting worse. We needed to get the tools to fix the starting mechanism and get out of here. We could not wait for hours for someone else to help us.

At least we had tools. The problem with my snowmobile was that the compartment was too small to handle tools and the emergency first aid kit that held the matches. This is why the emergency kit was in my wife's snowmobile. My wife and I had gone snowmobiling a week ago and we had both tools and a first aid kit. I carried the tools; she carried the emergency first aid kit. I was the mechanic and she was the nurse.

I thought that it would be easier now to go to my snowmobile. Jack and I had crawled back and forth a couple of times and there was beginning to be a semblance of a trail. As I started back, there was a new pool that had opened right in the middle of our trail. As I crawled to make a new trail on the side, I noticed that two other pools had opened along the way.

Where we had driven in and made tracks with the snowmobiles, the supporting ice underneath was weakened. Pools were opening all along the trail. I had to crawl all the way back to my snowmobile breaking a new trail in the powder snow. My body was telling me that this was hopeless. It was too far to go. I would not make it. I had no energy to continue.

When I finally got back, we worked about a half-hour on Irv's snowmobile. It was too dark to see a thing that we were doing. My hands were totally useless. I was shaking so badly that I could not hold anything. All of the dampness from my gloves, socks, and suit turned to ice and my hands were frozen along with my legs and feet. My hands and feet were unquestionably in trouble being so cold and numb.

Irv's hands were now numb from the unbearable cold. Because of this, he was having trouble handling a wrench or pliers. We were afraid that in the dark, if we got a part off, we might drop it and not find it in the snow due to our numb hands.

We ran into another problem. This new snowmobile was from Japan and had bolts that were metric. There were four metric bolts holding the starter mechanism on. My wrench kit was SAE that is common on American made products. We did have an adjustable wrench but it was rather large and cumbersome for the small bolts. Our numb hands and the darkness made it difficult just to adjust the wrench to fit the bolts.

It took us a while to get the four bolts off. This mechanism was really different then the ones on our other two snowmobiles. We had taken off the mechanism on the other snowmobiles and were familiar with how they worked. We had never seen this new improved type before. We couldn't even guess how this mechanism worked. Due to the darkness, we couldn't tell if a part broke or if it was just the rope that broke.

We took the mechanism back down to where my snowmobile was and started the snowmobile so that the headlight would work. What a total exhausting trip this was! We were unfamiliar with the workings of this mechanism. It seemed as though the part where the rope fastened had broken but we did not see any loose parts. A broken part could have dropped into the snow when Irv got the mechanism off.

After working diligently, we decided that it was useless. We were both numb and not thinking correctly. I think that this was one of our most serious problems. Our brains were freezing and not functioning properly. We were college degree, master degree men but our brains were lacking intelligence that was needed.

We both knew we were facing a grave problem. We just could not keep working like this in the bitter cold without any success. The freezing cold was creeping upon us gradually. The dangerous thing was that our brains were unable to detect this. A breeze was blowing and the wind chill was terrible. Our bodies were slowly freezing to death. We had to do something or face the inevitable.

Because Irv did not have his heavy snowmobile suit on, he was losing control of his mind. I was spewing out orders to a smart intelligent man because his mind was having trouble grasping at thoughts. My situation was grave. I was now in a frozen state with my hands, legs, and feet and was shaking uncontrollably. I have been frozen and shaking now for about three hours.

CHAPTER 10

<u>Failed Opportunities</u>

CHAPTER 10

It was now around 7:00 p.m. We had been working hard for three hours trying to get something working. We had been very serious because we knew that this was life threatening. We had to get out of there. We began thinking that if we kept moving; our bodies would warm up.

We decided to climb toward the top of the hill in Jack's tracks and maybe we follow his foot trail and make it to a mine shack that we had passed a couple of miles down the hill. Here, we would at least have shelter from the bitter breeze that was blowing.

As we started out, it was impossible to move in the thick powder. We made it about half way back to Irv's snowmobile and Irv said that he just could not make it. He said that he had no energy left. In a way, I was glad that he said this because with my numb legs, I could not feel anything when I took a step. I figured that one of my legs would snap off since they were frozen. My knees were not working either due to my frozen joints. The only way that I could get anywhere was to crawl and drag my legs.

This was getting impossible due to altitude and strength. It is hard to function at timberline and above with about half the oxygen that we were used to. We were over two miles up from sea level. We were also weak and about sick due to the lack of nourishment.

We were completely exhausted. We talked and said that there was only one thing left. We had to figure out a way to get my snowmobile out. It was working fine. We inched our way back to my machine. As we talked, we decided that it would be impossible to get through the box canyon and through the thick forest.

At least my snowmobile was working properly. If only we could get it out or around the pools of water, we could make it. I thought that Jack sure would be surprised to see us coming on my machine.

I had a terrible struggle getting back to my snowmobile. My legs and feet were frozen and numb as well as my arms and hands. My mind was slowing.

I had a lack of nourishment, and virtually no oxygen. Irv was behind me but moving very slowly. He was suffering but proud enough not to show it.

We lay in the snow a few minutes after reaching my snowmobile trying to replenish our lungs with oxygen and getting some strength back. My fingers were frozen and numb. They felt like clubs with no feeling. I had a terrible time just turning the key and pulling the starter rope to get the machine started. I had to use both hands to hold onto the rope. When the engine started, it was such a great sound! We had been trying so hard to get an engine to run.

I got on the snowmobile and tried to go toward the direction of the opening of the canyon. The water on top of the pools was freezing. I thought that I could try somehow to get around the pools on the left. There was only about a foot and one half of solid snow to work with at the side of the pool. I needed at least three feet. The problem that I was facing was that the edge of the pool on the right was a sharp drop down about three feet into water and ice. On the left was an 80-degree vertical hill.

Irv thought that if I could keep my weight on the left side of the machine with the left ski going upon the side of the wall, I might get through if I could go through with good speed. Keeping your weight over at the same side of a steep hill is very difficult. Irv thought that due to my height, I might be able to lean out and keep my weight shifted to the hillside.

I would have to make sure that the right ski was on solid snow or ice. If it did not work, I would turn the machine over on me into the pool of water. This would be a gamble that would probably be fatal for me if it did not work. This would be fatal for me because I could not get any more of my body in a frozen condition. Fatal, also, because the snowmobile might end on top of me in the deep pool and I might drown.

The way I felt at this time, I did not care. We decided that, at least, there was a small chance it might work. We were running out of ideas. We were at wit's end on other ways to get out using a snowmobile to get out of this frozen valley.

I hit full throttle to start moving the machine forward to get it on top of the snow. All of a sudden, the machine reared up like a car does when it is in neutral and it sank back into the powder. I had broken a drive belt! This is a belt that looks like an auto fan belt except it is two or three times wider. It goes from the engine to the transmission.

Thank goodness I always carried an extra! We have broken many drive belts so we always carried a spare with each snowmobile. We worked and worked trying to get the new belt on. A new belt is always hard to get on the drive pulleys even when warm. This is because it has not stretched out with wear and is tighter then an old one on the pulleys. We found that in this extreme cold temperature, the belt was like steel. It did not have any give. It needed to be stretched to get it on the pulley. With our cold hands, there was just no way to stretch it. Even though we were at the stage of freezing and we needed to get the belt on, our bodies just would not let us do it.

I laid the belt on the exhaust of the snowmobile trying to get it to soften up. This would not work. Our hands were so cold that we could not even hold a screwdriver. How could we get this drive belt on? We worked and worked. Irv, being the strong arm, tried but was unable to budge this belt.

It was about 7:30 p.m. We couldn't keep going like this with failed opportunities. Every time we failed, our bodies were dropping in temperature and getting closer to death. We were getting desperate with the cold. Even if we spent more time, chances of making it by the pool were very slim and dangerous. With the belt on, we would have nowhere to go.

Our slow thinking brains determined that just plain survival was all that was left. Our brains turned to simple life survival since it was twenty degrees below zero or less and we were both freezing to death. Irv went over into the trees and started digging a snow cave.

While he was doing this, I thought that I would try to figure out a way to start a fire. We needed a fire and, yet we had no matches. I had a snowmobile manual in the compartment of my machine. I got it out and tore out a page. I started the machine and pulled a spark plug wire off one of the two cylinders and got a beautiful one-inch spark! I held the paper to the spark and it went straight through scorching it but the paper would not catch fire. I tried to blow on it to get the spark to ignite but it would not work. I tried it on the edge as well as the middle and nothing.

I put some gasoline into one of our empty soda cans from the gas tank. Surely, by saturating the paper with gasoline, I could get a fire started. After trying and trying, I just could not get the spark to ignite the gasoline and paper! The spark would just dry the gasoline off the paper!

I yelled out to Irv to see if he had any ideas. He got me pine needles, tree bark, and cloth. Nothing worked! We both had been Boy Scouts. If this organization had seen this, they would have taken our fire starting badges away.

It was terrible to see that huge spark and never get a flame. Irv, a Denver Fireman and paramedic, made the comment "In Denver, when we do not want a fire, a smaller spark than that will ignite a building, but up here when we want a fire, nothing happens!"

We supposed that due to the bitter cold temperature and high altitude, gasoline must not vaporize as quickly. Also, we thought that since this gasoline had an oil mix, maybe this caused a problem. We could not understand why the snowmobile would start so easy and yet we could not get a flame.

The only difference we could guess at was that there was a chamber in the engine where the gas exploded. If we could make a chamber somehow, maybe we would have success. I took a rag and sprinkled it with gasoline and wadded it up to make a vapor chamber but it still would not work. At this point I was putting gas on everything. I was so cold that I did not care if there was a total explosion. In fact, I was thinking that a nice forest fire would be great about now.

We had to get heat from somewhere or freeze to death. I thought that the snowmobile engine would generate enough heat to give us some warmth. Maybe we could huddle around it until help arrived like huddling around a fire.

I started the engine and but couldn't find warmth anywhere. The exhaust manifold did not seem to give off much heat. I thought that the exhaust coming out might warm our hands. I tipped the machine on its side and held my numb hands in front of the exhaust pipe. It was warm, but the snowmobile has a two-cycle engine that requires oil to be mixed with the gasoline. As the oil burned off, going through the exhaust, a slight mist came out. This made my hands wet and with the slight breeze blowing, my hands just got colder.

I guess that this was another nice try with no success. We had to come up with something! We were running out of precious time. The bitter cold was killing us. Our physical bodies were shutting down and our mental state was getting worse because of dehydration and hypothermia.

CHAPTER 11

<u>Snow Cave</u>

CHAPTER 11

It was 8:00 p.m. and we had been stranded for four hours. My legs, feet, and hands were frozen for most of this time. My legs had no feeling. The aching that had been so severe in my legs was diminishing. I guess that it was taken over by the numbness.

I was having a bitter feeling--maybe a cold numb feeling. I knew in my mind that by the time help arrived and I got to a hospital, I would have run out of time to save my legs and hands. The bitter cold and stronger breeze was beginning to take its toll. I was still shaking and had been for all of the four hours. My snowmobile suit was normally warm especially with a sweater underneath. With the dampness and the ice coating, it did not seem that it was doing its job. I was better off then Irv who was having a real problem with his light jump suit.

Knowing that I had a severe medical condition that was probably irreversible, I offered my sweater to Irv. I figured that most of me was probably a goner anyway. He refused. I forgot that he was the "strong" one.

Irv and I knew that just keeping alive was all that was important especially not knowing whether Jack would get down the mountain. In fact, we were rather demoralized because we were pretty sure that it was impossible for Jack to crawl eight miles to the pickup. Like us, he did not have the strength left to crawl for very long. It probably took most of his remaining energy to fight several feet of powder snow up the hill. How could he go all that distance to the pickup? We were talking how Irv got hopelessly got stuck in two to three feet of powder just a short way from the pickup. How in the world could Jack crawl all that way without snowshoes?

All we could hope for now was that our wives would call the State Patrol and tell them that we had not returned. Our wives knew that we were going to Hall Valley. Hopefully, help was on its way. The big issue here is that it would probably be daybreak or later before we saw someone.

I have frozen hands and feet and they have now been frozen for several hours. Irv was in terrible shape physically and mentally. He was not thinking correctly due to how frozen he had been for so long. My thinking was also getting impaired. I was having trouble thinking out what we needed to do. I was sure that there was something that we missed doing to help out our situation. My competitive brain would not stop thinking how to get out of this.

We had endured the freezing temperature for so long and also had been under so much stress, it was taking its toll. Irv's brain was starting to communicate to his physical body that maybe everything was okay. It was telling him that he were not in as bad a shape as he thought. My brain was sure not telling me that I was warm. The shaking of my body was terrible.

We had reminded Jack about the mining shack a couple of miles downhill. At least it had a roof. It would be terribly cold inside with the breeze blowing through the open windows and door. Before Jack left, we told him that if he could not go further, he should hole up there until help would arrive. It was tough for Irv and me to think about the old cabin. We knew that Jack should at least save himself. He probably did stop there and the chance of our rescue was slim to none.

It seemed as though all possibilities of escaping down the mountain or getting warm were exhausted. We had been trying to get out for over four hours seeking warmth. We felt that our only chance of survival was that a search party might come. As cold as we were, both of us knew that our chance of survival through the night was probably impossible. We were weak, hungry, exhausted, cold, and mentally ill. We couldn't escape the cold. It gets on your mind and it gets worse. When you are facing death or if at best, being in a wheel chair the rest of your life, it is hard to stay positive. We had to try something, anything, to get warm.

We knew that when buried in snow the temperature would be about thirty-two degrees. This would be about fifty degrees warmer then we are now. Wow, a warm thirty-two degrees—right at freezing! At least, this would put the odds of survival a little more in our favor even though I had already determined that I had lost both of my legs and possibly my hands. Irv had been digging in a drift about four feet deep in the trees. He was trying to dig a snow cave. It was like trying to make a snowman in powder snow! It was impossible. He tried and tried to no avail.

We thought about breaking branches off the trees and making a shelter but our hands was too cold and useless and we were too exhausted. By the time we could get a hut of branches made and pile snow on it, another hour or two would go by with both of us freezing worse then now.

We pushed ourselves into Irv's drift, feet and legs first, so that just our faces were exposed. We knew that this was not the way to do a snow cave, but it was the best we could do under the circumstances. We thought that if we warmed up a little in the balmy thirty-two degree grave we were in and got some strength back, we could try to make a better shelter later.

By now, it was after 8:00 p.m., and we were unbearably cold. My legs were numb and my arms were aching almost to the point of making me scream. When you cannot escape discomfort, you panic. Your mind does crazy things. I was having hallucinations about being warm. I was having trouble just lying there. Surely something else could be done.

What made it worse was that I remembered reading about people freezing to death and how they at some point started feeling comfortably warm. The brain just doesn't understand the cold and finally tells you that it must be okay. I knew that I was freezing to death and I needed to do something to turn things around. It could be many hours before help arrived and something needed to change.

Lying in this tomb seemed as if we had just given up. Maybe it was true and it was making me disgusted. With my competitive nature, I had never given up on anything in my life. We had tried so many things and everything failed. This competitive nature was now the issue that needed to be solved. There had to be something that we could do. The trouble was that my brain was thinking so slowly that I could not think straight. Panic was beginning to creep into our dilemma.

When panic seeps into your mind, you want to run. As an athlete, running had always been easy. The thought of running or walking out flashed through my mind again but this was impossible with my frozen feet and Irv's heavy weight. For me to walk out was like driving at sixty miles per hour with four flat tires. This was an impossible situation!

I continued weighing different things thinking that there was surely something that we had not tried.

We must try every possibility! Finally, the four-five hours of panic stopped. I so was so mentally tired from the constant thinking about how to get out of there that I just had to let go. How could I be a competitor and let go? I was freezing cold, starving, exhausted, and mentally tired.

We just settled down in our snow bed and looked at the stars hoping that something might happen. It was comforting to just lay there and rest. We had not had anything comforting since we got here. But, I couldn't get comfortable because I was shaking uncontrollably. With the shakes, I was having trouble keeping the powder snow off my face. Every time I would shake, the snow would fall from where we had it piled up.

It was a fatalistic feeling to know that with every minute ticking by, pieces of my body were dying. I was sure that Irv was feeling the same way. Irv was in such bad shape that he got very quiet and reserved.

Lying in this state with my competitive spirit not giving up, I decided that we needed to talk to each other to keep awake since our brains were starting to tell us that our bodies were beginning to warm. I got Irv talking although he needed to be prodded.

It was difficult thinking of things to say. Our brains were muddled and Irv could not continue talking. It was up to me. I was not going to go down without a fight. I started reminiscing about my life story.

CHAPTER 12

<u>Sand Hills</u>

CHAPTER 12

Irv's family was from Nebraska and he told me about his dad living in poverty before coming to Colorado.

I told Irv that my dad also came from Nebraska. "He was born in the Sand Hills back in 1917. The Sand Hills, located in the western part of the state, are approximately 20,000 square miles of sand dunes. Some of these dunes reach several hundred feet in height. The dunes were covered in vegetation but with dryness around the edges you often could see sand. This sand moved with the ever-constant wind. The biggest parcels of land in Nebraska were found in the Sand Dunes. These were the vast cattle ranches. The area my dad lived was called the Bad Lands."

Hey! This was working. Irv started listening and his eyes opened and stayed open. He had an interest in Nebraska. I decided to continue on:

"My dad's father owned a general store in a remote small town in the Sand Hills. My dad as a tiny kid would sit on the porch of the store with his dad. He really enjoyed the middle of the day when there were very few people in town. Since there was no business to tend to, his dad would often sit in one of the old rockers on the porch of the store. He would shoot at the prairie dogs in the street with his Remington .22 rifle. As a little boy, my dad really thought that this was something!"

I knew that Irv would like the .22 rifle story because he had a large gun collection. We got in a conversation about what type of a .22 rifle it was.

I continued on: "My dad can remember people coming into the store complaining about the prairie dogs. They were everywhere and were a real curse to the town and the farmers in the Sand Hills. They would dig big, deep holes for their dens in the street or the side of the street. If a person did not watch where they were walking, they or their animals could have a sprained or broken ankle.

Out on the range, the ranchers were always on the lookout for these holes and rattlesnakes. The rattlesnakes thrived on the prairie dogs and were often in the prairie dog holes waiting for them. Ranchers were very careful when they walked the fields.

There was always danger lurking. When a rattlesnake bit a person in those days, it was often fatal because of a lack of medical help. My dad can remember the ranchers coming into the store with knee high rattlesnake proof leather boots.

Outside the store were thousands of spent short .22 cartridges from his dad's gun. A wholesale farm supplier would come by rail to the store once a month to see what his dad needed in supplies. The supplier told him that if he would sell Remington rifles, he would give him an unlimited supply of short .22 shells. This became his entertainment--shooting at the prairie dogs.

I asked my dad how the townspeople put up with the constant shooting. He said that the wind was blowing constantly and was noisy and most of the town probably didn't hear anything. He also said that the town did not like prairie dogs and they were probably happy that someone was getting rid of them. I am sure that the town realized that it was the prairie dogs that attracted rattlesnakes. My dad talked about people coming into the store remarking that some day, the main street would be paved with steel cartridges and the mud would be gone."

Since Irv was awake, I continued: "The store was a typical frame two-story building seen in many small towns on the plains. Inside it had a feeling of comfort and warmth with the pot-bellied stove. As my dad looked back, the store was just like the ones you see in the old western films.

Because he was so small, he was not allowed to go up the stairs to the second floor. He does not remember ever going up there but he remembers playing on the lower few stairs with his wooden cars. The stairs were at the left side of the store and went up behind the potbellied stove. Everyone hung out around the stove in the winter. Dad can remember the stove being unbearably hot at times and he would have to move elsewhere until the fire would burn down. He was happy when his dad used coal in the morning since it was a more stable constant heat. The store was on a corner lot. There was stairs that went to the second floor on the side of the building right behind the wall where the inside stairs were. Dad can remember playing on the inside stairs and hearing someone climbing the stairs on the outside.

Dad can still remember his dad putting on the tube records on the old Edison phonograph. He had boxes of records and ranchers from near and far would come in and sit by the stove and listen to old hymns, Eddie Cantor, Jimmy Durante and others.

He can also remember his dad listening to the old Philco radio on the counter by the cash register. He would listen intently so that he could hear the time to reset the wind-up Waterbury clock that sat on the shelf behind the counter. It had to be rewound every day and sometimes he would forget. He was always saying, "I need to wind the Waterbury." The radio was the only way of keeping up with the correct time.

My dad said that the Waterbury was so much fun when it would ring a bell at half past the hour and gong on the hour for the number of times for each hour. Dad would always hang around when it got to ten, eleven, or twelve in the morning. He was unhappy when he missed the many gongs and it was one or two o'clock in the afternoon. His dad and others would tell him when it was close to the hour so that he could hear the gong. They got a kick out of seeing him so excited."

I would like to say now that talking about by dad was now working but Irv was starting to doze. Now we have been buried for two hours and hope is diminishing. I knew that I needed to continue to talk not only for the hope that Irv would not go into a deep sleep but that I would not go to sleep. It would be easy right now to not worry about anything and just take a nap.

CHAPTER 13

<u>Arsonist</u>

CHAPTER 13

My tale continued hoping that Irv might listen. I started thinking about the terrible snowstorms my dad talked about in Nebraska. "The Sand Hill winters were devastating due to the terrible winds. It was cold and windy with the snowdrifts reaching the height of many of the buildings. There were virtually no trees on the sand hills but there were some in town that helped to break the snow—or the sand. At times, when the wind blew in the spring, his dad said that the sand would pile high up on the side of the buildings. He said that they would shovel it into the street to help with the mud and the ruts from the old black cars and trucks and some horse driven wagons. My dad can remember his parents stuffing rags into the cracks around the windows and doors to keep the sand from blowing in.

Speaking of ruts in the road, some ranchers would find that pulling a wagon with a team of horses would get them about anywhere. They would not get stuck in the ruts that were in all the roads like the cars would. He would enjoy watching these wagons go by the store. The ranchers would raise teams of horses just for pulling these wagons. There was a type of competition to see who had the best looking teams.

One problem was that the wagons with their narrow wheels would leave worse ruts that would make driving an automobile sometimes impossible. People were always coming out of the buildings and helping push someone out of a rut. Instead of calling it Main Street, they should have called it Rut Street.

Trying to get out of town was sometimes very difficult or maybe impossible. The outside roads were constantly changing with the winds and the sand. A good usable road yesterday sometimes would be covered with sand drifts and not be usable today. This made horse travel prominent in the area.

Dad can remember many people coming into the store and tying up their horse at one of the hitching posts just like in the old westerns. He can remember two hitching posts in front of the store. These posts had several steel rings bolted onto it to tie the horse.

At times, people would bring another horse or two to tie their goods onto for the trip home.

He does not remember people driving fancy buggies although the doctor, who was my dad's uncle, had one. He found that traveling from one end of the area to another was at times impossible especially for a car due to the wind and the sand. When returning from a far away call, the snow or the sand would drift across the road making travel impossible. Sometimes he would spend the night and wait for daybreak. There were several stories where he got stranded out on a sandy road and the ranchers would have to pull him out with their team of horses.

At the store, the potbellied stove was the gathering place for town meetings and town gossip. Chairs and benches were brought in and the bean barrels would be pushed back along with other store goods to make room. Dad can remember, later, hearing about legal matters being resolved here.

This probably was the first courthouse in the area. My dad does not remember who the judge was. His dad knew everyone in the territory. I wouldn't be surprised if he was a type of judge in those days. Dad never heard about anybody being hanged. This was such a remote area that there was very little crime. If there were, it would be difficult to get away. Al the ranchers worked in harmony with each other and pretty well knew what was going on around them.

My granddad's checkerboard had been used so much that the squares were getting hard to see. He would often use a pencil to color in the black squares. My dad had trouble telling what square a person was playing on. He was not sure that they knew either. This probably added to the fun, although he did not understand how they could have fun with a board and some round pieces of wood.

My granddad must have been the checker champ in the valley. Men were always challenging him for a game. My dad remembers men coming in and spending all afternoon playing a game. Either no one was ever in a hurry or nobody could see the squares.

In those days, the town did not have electricity. It was too far out into the hills and it cost too much to stretch electrical lines that far. There were poles by the railroad tracks that stretched telephone lines. The town only had one telephone and it was at my granddad's store. It was a wood one that hung on the wall with an attached mouthpiece and an earphone on a cord. Most of the time, the lady operator at the other end was gone. My dad can remember his dad complaining that if there were an emergency, there would be no one at the other end of the line.

Because the Santa Fe and Burlington railroad came through the valley, the town was told that electricity would be put in as soon as money was available for poles and lines. The town was becoming a major railroad stop since there was such a great need for the transportation of cattle. At times, my dad would not see a train for weeks because the sand or snow would drift over the tracks.

Sand controlled the existence of life. It was on everything and in everything, even the food. My dad's family was used to the crunch of sand when they ate. Years later, my granddad salted his ice cream saying that he was used to having sand in it.

The railroad stop had several corals and chutes for cattle and sheep to be put into waiting to be loaded into the rail cars going to Omaha.

The town was miles from any other town and these were also small. The railroad was the main means of transportation to get to the next town. If people did not use the rail, they came by horse during those days because the roads were either washed out or covered by sand.

Not having electricity created a serious problem at dad's home on top of the hill in the Sand Hills. This house was constantly fighting wind and sand. His dad would paint the house and the sand would grind the paint off.

Because the house was on the hill, most of the sand or snow would blow around it and go down into the town. The back of the house would always have a five or six-foot drift of snow and sand piled up against the outside wall. This made going out to the privy an adventure especially in the winter.

They had coal oil lamps to light the house. They also had an outside coal oil lamp that lit the way for someone coming up the hill. This lamp was hard to keep lit due to the constant wind.

One deadly incident happened when dad was crawling around the home at one and one-half years old. He could pull himself up at the couch or a chair but he was not walking yet. He crawled into the living room from the kitchen where his mother was cooking supper. He pulled himself up at the table that had a lit oil lamp on it. When he tried to stand up, he grabbed the tablecloth. The tablecloth slid off the table sending the lamp over his head. The lamp dropped to the floor with a crash. As the lamp broke, a large fire broke out consuming the rug and then the drapes. Fortunately, the oil did not get on him.

His mother heard the crash and her son crying. She ran into the room horrified when she saw the flame! She grabbed him with one hand and tried her best with her other hand to snuff it out with a blanket but it was spreading too fast. All she could do was grab my dad and get out of the house.

All the buildings in the area were a frame construction. If a fire started, it burned rapidly. My dad's mother ran to the neighbor's house screaming and the neighbor ran down the hill to the store. The neighbor ran into the store and told my granddad that his house was on fire on the hill. He ran up the hill terrified about the safety of his family. This was just one of the prices to pay living in a remote area.

Not even two years old and dad had burned the family house. He was pretty young to have an arsonist, juvenile record!"

Irv began stirring again as I reminisced about Nebraska. Maybe it was working. It was now about three hours that we had been buried.

CHAPTER 14

<u>Horse Buggy</u>

CHAPTER 14

I told Irv that I enjoyed my dad telling some of these nostalgic stories from the past. Some were neat and then there were others. Some things that happened often resulted in tragedy. One such instance involved my granddad's brother-in-law who was the doctor.

"The town's doctor was a very intelligent man who earned a scholarship to a medical school back east. He was raised in Council Bluffs, Iowa, just across the river from Omaha, Nebraska. He knew about the Sand Hills and often traveled through the area because of his love for the land and the people.

After graduation from medical school, he came back home and opened a practice in Council Bluffs. When his brother, my granddad, moved to the Sand Hills from Council Bluffs, he got an itching to go to the Sand Hills and set up practice there. A year later, he did so, moving into the second floor of my granddad's store. Now the town and the "Bad Lands" had a doctor. He practiced there for twenty-five years delivering babies and helping with sickness, bone breaks, and snake bites.

One blustery, cold winter night, a foreman of a large ranch 15 miles south of town rode his horse into town and asked the doctor if he could hurry out to the ranch. The owner's wife was in labor and something was terribly wrong. The foreman told the doctor that the road was getting impassible due to drifts. The foreman offered to drive the doctor but the doctor told him to get back and tell them that he was on his way.

The doctor decided that he would take his buggy. There was snow blowing and drifting and he knew that his car would not make it. He harnessed his horse to the buggy and took off towards the ranch. He was concerned because he had delivered this young mother to be when he first came to the area. So this was like taking care of family.

He never came home. The next morning, he was found dead on the road. His wrecked buggy was up the road about a quarter of a mile from his body. His horse was still tethered to it.

People in the area said that it looked as if he got caught in a drift of sand and snow. They thought that maybe he had gotten out to push and lift the buggy through the drift and had a heart attack.

This was a terrible, devastating thing to happen to this area. The doctor was known by all and would be sorely missed. A doctor was a rich commodity in areas like this. He probably would not be replaced because the region was so remote and hard to live in."

Irv did listen to this story and told me not to tell depressing stories. I realized that during the time I told this story, my thoughts went from my frozen body to the story. It was a relief to get my mind elsewhere.

CHAPTER 15

<u>World War II</u>

.

CHAPTER 15

I thought that I needed to find something to talk about that dealt with me. "I can remember at two years of age, my daddy being absent from home. Something just wasn't right. My daddy who often played with me was gone. The Army had taken him away. My mother said that he got drafted. He left on the Santa Fe-Burlington Railroad and my mother cried for hours afterwards. Something was wrong and strange in my world.

My mother packed all of our things and we left our rented house and moved in with her parents. We had gotten word that my dad's dad had come down with tuberculosis in Nebraska. He was in not good shape and was told by a doctor that he needed to leave the Sand Hills because of the sand and dust in his lungs.   He would be joining us later when his properties were sold.

In my new world, I would sit for hours on the curb in front of my grandpa's house in Denver and watch the cars and trucks drive by. I had lived in a small town and this was exciting.

I could sense my mother's sadness worrying about my daddy in the Army and my granddad in the Sand Hills. On top of this, my daddy's brother signed up for the Air Force because he feared being drafted. He was going somewhere east for basic training in the special service division.   He would eventually be stationed at Lowry Air Force Base in Denver, as the commanding general's secretary. My uncle could type faster then anyone in his high school. He used this skill to keep from being shipped overseas. When my uncle left for basic training, he left a wife and son.

This disruption in our lives gave me a feeling of uncertainty and I would often cry not knowing why. Every day there was talk about someone's loved ones that were killed in the war.   There was a cloud of darkness and desperation over everyone because of the waiting.

I can remember my mother's sister living in a small cottage on my grandparent's property. She had two daughters. Her husband had been drafted by the Navy and was on a ship somewhere out on the Pacific Ocean.

I constantly heard people talking about the war--something that I was too young to understand. My mother would often cry herself to sleep not knowing if my dad, his brother, or her sister's husband would return alive from this terrible war.

Thousands of young men and women never came back from the Pacific or Europe. Many just disappeared with no record and no witness of where they had been killed.

My aunt was a great support to my mother. The two sisters would sit for hours and talk about their husbands and the war. They were writing letters every day. They would run to the mailbox when the mailman came to see if there was mail from their husbands. They would read each other's letters over and over crying as they did so.

I can remember playing on the floor in my grandparent's living room in the evenings and listening with them to the large console radio. This is when people across our nation would get all the daily information about the war with Germany and Japan. We would be listening to programs such as Bob Hope,

Fibber McGee and Molly, Jack Benny, or The Shadow. I remember my mother laughing and being so happy then someone would break in with a war bulletin and the seriousness and sadness would return. I would often climb onto the big sofa and lay in my mother's lap to console her after the bulletins because I could sense that something was seriously wrong.

At night and during my afternoon naps, I would have nightmares about the Germans and the Japanese coming to our city. In my dreams, I would have to run and hide. I would awaken with a start and start crying. At times when I was sitting in the bathroom, waiting for bodily functions to happen, my mind would often wander about the Germans. When I heard a sound, I thought the enemy was invading our house. I would start crying. My mother would have to come in to console me. She would ask me what was wrong but I couldn't answer her. She was confused about why I was crying. Being as young as I was, I did not know how to explain why I was crying. I just knew that she would make everything right.

During the WW II days, emotions were rampant due to the unknown everywhere. Our country and the freedom that we had were in jeopardy of

changing to a country being controlled by Hitler. I
could sense the anxiety of my family."

CHAPTER 16

<u>Hypothermia</u>

CHAPTER 16

After midnight, all hope was fading that help would arrive on time. It had been about eight hours since I fell into the freezing pool. My feet and legs had been frozen for almost all of this time and it was turning colder because of a stiff breeze. The breeze was unbearable, cutting into my face like needles. It was very hard just doing nothing! I knew my hands and legs were frozen and dead. It was hard not being totally demoralized. My mind kept dwelling on one of two things that could happen. I would freeze to death or, if I was rescued, I would spend the rest of my days in a bed or a wheel chair. This was a terrible thing to face especially since I had such a beautiful wife. We enjoyed each other very much and were expecting to lead a wonderful married life with the possibility of children. I had a feeling of shame come over me for doing this to my wife.

Irv was now in a deep sleep. He was still alive because he was snoring loudly. It looks as if telling him my life story was too much for him to bear. I knew that my story was not that interesting but to put someone to sleep? This would hurt anyone's ego!

It had been a while since I had tried to drink water and I knew that water was necessary to remain hydrated. Hypothermia was taking over our bodies. I knew that hypothermia becomes evident when body temperature starts dropping.   My constant shaking since I fell in the water was reminding me that I was experiencing this dreaded condition.

Earlier, Irv had filled our empty soda cans with icy cold water from the pool. Drinking icy water when I was freezing to death was not something that made me comfortable.   I felt that the water was freezing me on the inside and down to my stomach. Since the icy water made us colder, we just did not drink any more. Lying in this frozen tomb, I did not want to venture out into the cold to go to the pool to drink icy water.

Trying to be prepared for snowmobiling, Erv and I had read how hypothermia was very dangerous.

It kills some people before they freeze to death. We were concerned about it but what could we do? Death can become a real possibility if hypothermia persists for more then a few hours. It had been at least eight hours. I tried not to dwell on the hypothermia issue. I knew that I had it and thinking about it was doomsday thinking. What concerned me was that hypothermia just might be killing me and I didn't know it. I might pass out or just go to sleep with certain death. Since Irv was already sleeping, I would have no one to awaken me. We would both be goners. This was another thing that was nerve racking.

I was having trouble talking due to the extreme cold. I was slurring my words terribly and Irv had been having the same problem. I knew that my lips and face were half frozen but I could tell that my brain was also not allowing me to communicate properly. Was I just freezing or was this hypothermia?

A medical doctor later told me that once you have used the storage of energy in your body, the drop in body temperature causes a gradual physical and mental slow down. We had not eaten all day! How much energy did I have? The doctor told me that a person might not notice the slow down but they can see it in others. I saw it in Irv. He was clumsy, sleepy, irritable, had slurred speech, and he was very confused. It got to the point where I could not get him to help me because he was so irritable. I did not want Irv to be irritable. He was physically strong and I did not want his strength out of control. Was I the same way? What had Irv seen in me that was not quite right?

When I was trying to start the fire with the snowmobile engine spark, Irv just stood there not saying anything. I needed him to help but he couldn't. I felt bad because he had on the light jumpsuit and did not complain once. I explained to him that he needed to go over and dig a snow cave for us. He did not understand. I pointed towards the trees and tried to guide him there. Being this proud man of great physical strength, I was sure that he was having trouble being ordered around.

I was in dire need of something--anything to get warm and thaw out my limbs. It was getting impossible to make Irv understand anything that I was saying. Our communication was fading. This was just another problem that surfaced--a problem that was telling me that we needed help now. We did not have much time. It was unbearable having frozen limbs but now our heads and brains were not functioning properly.

The only thing that I knew to do was to try talking even though I was hard to understand. It was hard trying to use my lips and tongue to voice my words. I could tell that my face was having serious problems. I was beginning to worry that my eyes would start freezing. Being buried, there was virtually no movement going on with my body. I had to keep my mind working. I continued my muddled talking.

CHAPTER 17

<u>West Point</u>

.

CHAPTER 17

"My dad had a terrible time as a kid. He had Rheumatic fever when he was seventeen. He was in bed with this fever for a whole year and the doctor told his parents that he would eventually die. My dad's heart had swollen the size of three men's hearts. His chest was bulging from the swelling. The doctor said that this much stress on the walls of the heart muscle would be fatal. He was so terribly weak that he could not sit up in bed and had trouble turning over on his side. His parents had to live day by day knowing that his heart was ready to burst any minute.

Every night they prayed with him for healing. They would kiss his forehead before leaving the room realizing that the next morning he probably would be gone. He had terrible pain in his legs day after day. One night, my dad was able to doze off for a while when the aspirin went to work. He woke and his dad was standing at the foot of the bed with tears streaming down his cheeks. My dad said that he would never forget this image.

After the year in bed, he started getting stronger little by little. The swelling of his heart went down. He started sitting in a chair and doing some walking around the house. The doctor told his parents that he was glad to see the improvement but nothing was changed. The doctor gave him a maximum two years to live due to the damage that had been done to his heart walls by this terrible disease. The doctor still thought that his heart would burst any moment since it was beating at a very irregular rate.

This irregular rate was taking a toll on him every day. He would get so exhausted that he would spend most of the day lying down on the sofa.

My mother had been dad's girlfriend at church before he got sick. They had known each other for years. They both sang in the youth choir with my dad's brother. When my dad started improving and going back to school and church, they talked about marriage. They wanted to spend as much time as possible with each other before he died. The doctor told them that he hated to put a damper on the romance but it was a serious mistake getting married because he would not live. He said that it would "taint" my mother and make it harder for her to find someone else.

Everyone tried to discourage them from getting married. They would tell them that it was not fair for my mother. To marry and then to lose a husband that soon would ruin her life. But, one year later, after my mother graduated from high school, they got married.

My dad was worried that when he graduated, the Army would come after him. Our nation was on the brink of World War II. The military was drafting many young men for training just in case of war. Our president was looking at how World War I had taken such a huge toll on our nation and he wanted to be prepared just in case.

My dad thought that being an officer would be easier then starting at the lowest rank. He applied to Officer Candidate School at the Army's recruitment center. Two weeks later, he received a letter from the Army with a form to fill out with personal and medical information. When he saw the medical questions, he knew that he would not be considered because of his heart failure. He sent the form to the

Army and a quick letter came back saying that he had been denied due to his medical condition. They said that he was "Unfit for military service." His dad thought this was good because he probably wouldn't be drafted.

His school principal told him that he should apply at West Point because of his extremely good grades. The principal said that he would contact a senator who would help my dad with the application for the appointment. The principal told him that if he was accepted, it would take four years to graduate and the war would probably be through.

My dad would have an appointment if his application and physical were accepted. His application came back denied again. My dad's doctor told him that even if his application had been accepted, when my dad reported for the physical, his irregular heartbeat and his past medical history would have washed him out.

My dad did not have money for college since the family savings was totally used up taking care of his illness. His grades were outstanding in high school but scholarships during that day were hard to come by. My mother was working as a secretary but her paycheck was not enough for them. He needed to work also to support them both.

He got a job at Montgomery Ward. He got off at 2:00 a.m. and would sleep on the streetcar bench in front of the store. The conductor would stop and yell to wake him up to get on the car. He would go to the back of the streetcar and go to sleep on the wide back window bench. It was quiet since there was no one else on the car early in the morning. When the streetcar got to the end of the line where he needed to get off, the conductor would wake him.

These hours became a burden to him and his failing health. He talked to his brother who had driven a taxi for some time before he entered the service. Dad drove taxi for several months until he got hit on the head from behind one night and robbed.

My granddad worked for a furniture company as an accountant. He called my dad and told him the company needed some part time help. But, doing something physical was out of the question. The owner of the furniture store had been very supportive to my granddad during my dad's illness. He had given my granddad time off when needed for doctor's appointments and other medical essentials.

My granddad talked to the owner and explained that he needed a job with little or no physical labor. He said that my dad needed someone with patience to hire him. He needed a break from someone because he might not live much longer! He told him that my dad had tried to work but was still struggling with strength issues. The owner hired my dad and told him to work a little at a time and try to do more each day. He told my dad that the company had plenty of sofas in stock and he was welcome to use them when customers weren't there.

Dad worked a little at a time doing janitorial services and seemed to be getting stronger daily. At times, trucks would come full of furniture so he started helping a little unloading the trucks. If he got tired, he would rest a while before continuing. The truck drivers knew that my dad had very little time left and were very careful with him. They didn't want him dying on their shift.

After a few months, his strength got somewhat better. He started loading furniture into the truck and going out on deliveries as a helper. One day, the driver quit and my dad took over driving the truck and having his own helper.

It had now been four years since he got out of bed with his sickness. He was two years over the maximum time given him by the doctors. He and my mother often talked about having a family but were still not sure of my dad's future. One day, they decided to try to have children of which I am the youngest of two. Friends and family told them that they were crazy to even consider raising a family. The kids would soon lose their dad."

CHAPTER 18

<u>Battle of the Bulge</u>

CHAPTER 18

"In 1943 when I was one and one half years old, my dad got another letter from the Army. This was a draft letter saying to report to Camp Roberts Army Base in California, south of Los Angeles. My parents were devastated to think how he was turned away twice from the Army and now they were drafting him.

My dad took letters to the draft board from heart specialists stating that he would die in training. He also took the denial letters from the Officer Candidate School and West Point showing that he was unfit for military service. His doctor also wrote the draft board saying that he should not be drafted because he would not survive basic training. It did not matter. The Army was in need of warm bodies to

167

fight the war. They were taking anyone if they were breathing and could walk.

Dad went through basic training for a couple of months. It was terribly difficult because he had no stamina. Even though he struggled, he seemed to be treated fairly. The Army personnel had seen his letters and were fairly sympathetic toward his predicament. He was last place in many of the drills but was never reprimanded for being behind because he always finished. He never had to do KP where the slackers ended up.

At the end of basic training, the troop took a final hike called a five-mile speed hike. This is where the soldiers would trot for five miles without stopping while carrying a full pack and rifle. Dad was trotting beside his bunk partner who became his good friend. This man was 6'2" and 354 lbs. This overweight fellow was too heavy and out of shape to do anything. He spent most of his time on KP duty because he could not finish a lot of the drills. He could not carry a full backpack on a walking five-mile hike. There was no way he could trot.

After the first mile, his friend collapsed and could not continue. They were towards the back of the file and the sergeant was leading at the front. Dad worked quickly and took a canteen of water and splashed it on his friend's face. Then he grabbed his friend's pack. He told him to rest and catch up as quickly as he could and stay at the end of the file. This was to keep the sergeant off their back. My dad unbelievably carried his friend's pack with his own and finished the hike.

The next day after they finished the hike, my dad became very ill and was put into the infirmary. He was on the edge of heart failure. Did this matter to the military? No! He was readied to leave for war the next week.

Basic training was through and it was time to move the soldiers by train from Los Angeles to Maryland. The Army was in a rush to get them to a waiting ship to take them to Belgium. They were going to Belgium to fight in what was later called "The Battle of the Bulge." This battle was taking place on the border of Belgium and Germany in the Ardennes Forest. When the battle started, the weather turned to sub-zero degrees for the remainder of the battle.

This would become the most deadly battle of World War II for the Allies. This battle came after the terrible Normandy, France battle where the Allies suffered so many casualties.

The Battle of the Bulge started December 16, 1944, and ended January 25, 1945. This was the largest land battle of World War II in which the United States participated. More than a million men fought in this battle that included 600,000 Germans, 500,000 Americans, and 55,000 British. At the conclusion of the battle the casualties were as follows: 81,000 Americans with 19,000 killed, 1,400 British with 200 killed, and 100,000 Germans killed, wounded or captured.

By this time in the war, the German Army did not have the reserves that Allies had waiting. Because of lack of troops for Germany, this eventually would be the decisive battle of the war.

When he got to Maryland and on the ship, it was raining and had been doing so for over a week. It was cold and damp with no heat on the ship. Soldiers by the thousands were laid out with hardly any room to move on many floors of the shop. They were waiting for the ship to fill up with troops arriving from all over the country.

After a few nights in the damp, cold weather, my dad got deathly sick and was taken off the ship and put in an Army hospital. He had spent three days and nights on the ship. He was taken to Fort George Mead Hospital where he spent several weeks in bed where the prognosis was heart failure. Surprise, surprise!

The hospital found out that a general was coming to the hospital for an inspection. The patients had been forewarned by the hospital's commanding officer. The patients were given orders that when the general came into the room, they should get up out bed and stand at attention at the foot of the bed and salute. My dad told the commanding officer that the cardiologist had given him strict orders not to get out of bed, it might kill him. The commanding officer gave my dad a dirty look and looked at him thinking that he was being sarcastic. He was not used to someone questioning his orders. When an officer gave an order, no one questioned it without consequences. He grabbed my dad's chart that was attached on the foot of the bed. It said that my dad was in heart failure. He told my dad to lie stiff and salute when the general arrived. Then he told my dad that he would talk to his cardiologist. Dad could see that he did not trust him.

When the general came into the room, he stopped at dad's bed and looked at him a moment, smiled, and saluted him. Then he continued on with the inspection of the floor with a very stern look.

A week later, the cardiologist came to dad and told him that he was going to discharge him from active service. He said that he would die in the first fox hole that he would get into.

When the doctor was talking with my dad, he asked my dad if he had a family back home. My dad told him that he had a wife and two kids. The doctor told my dad that the nicest thing that he could do for him and his family was to send him home to die. He didn't want him to die in the hospital. "I just hope that you get there in time to see your wife and kids. I think it would be better for you to fly so that you will get there in time." The cardiologist discharged dad immediately after 6 months and 3 days in the Army.

Dad said that this doctor was really great and easy to talk with. He had a successful cardiologist practice in New York City and was drafted to serve at the army hospital there in Maryland. The doctor told him that he had a wife and kids and knew how important it was for my dad to see his family.

Dad left the hospital with a fever, chills, and no stamina. His heart was beating wildly and he had terrible chest pain. He wasn't sure that he would make it to the taxi in front of the hospital. He took the taxi to the airport to get a ticket. The taxi driver could tell he was sick. My dad told him that the Army discharged him from the hospital to go home to die. When he got to the airport, the taxi driver helped him into the terminal and carried his duffel bag for him. When my dad reached to get his wallet out to pay him, the taxi driver told him that the trip was on the house. He told dad that he hoped that he would be able get home in time to visit with his family.

After resting a while, dad got in line at the ticket counter and sat on his duffel bag because he thought that he would faint. After an hour of inching closer and closer, the ticket clerk asked if he was an officer or if he had a specialty. He told the woman that he wasn't an officer but he was special. She wasn't in the mood for a joke and asked for the next person.

He left the terminal and took a taxi to the railroad depot with the realization that he probably would not see his wife or kids. He was feeling weaker and weaker and was blacking out.

The train going nonstop from Maryland to Denver was full and they were not taking soldiers on it. He was told to go to Chicago and try to get a train from there to Denver. There was one ticket left. When he got on the train, he fell into a seat and immediately went to sleep. He slept the whole way to Chicago and was surprised that he was not dead when he got there.

He went to the ticket counter for a ticket to Denver. After another hour in line, inching little by little and sitting on his duffel bag, he asked if he could buy a ticket from Chicago to Denver. He was told that there were no tickets available except for officers. He told the clerk that he was sick and wanted to see his wife and kids before he died. The clerk did not respond and said "Whose next?" This clerk had probably heard a story like this several times a day.

There was a sailor sitting in a chair by the ticket line. He overheard the conversation my dad had with the clerk. He had been watching my dad inching along in the line looking white as a sheet. He could tell that he was sick.

He stopped my dad as he was walking by and asked my dad to follow him. He went to where several Army Military Police were sitting. They were all sergeants. The sailor told them the story that he overheard. One of sergeants went to the ticket counter and told them to issue him a ticket.

There were no seats available on the train. He had a boarding pass but no seat. He got on the train and started walking from car to car. He would wait for someone who was leaving to go to eat or go to the bathroom and he would sit in their seat until they came back. He went from car to car doing this until it got dark. People stopped moving around and were sleeping in their seats.

He found a spot to sit on the floor under a table in the bar car. Since it was dark, he tried to stretch out on the floor and sleep. Every hour or so a porter would walk through and tell him that he could not be on the floor. He would get up and move to another car then come back and go under another table and try to sleep some more. He was in heart failure and probably dying and he had to sit and sleep on the floor of a rail car from Chicago to Denver.

My mother and I were so excited to see him when he arrived home. I would not let him out of my sight. He had not been able to call my mother to tell her that he was coming home. Every time he would find a telephone, there would be a line of service men and women trying to make a call.

It was raining in Denver when he showed up at the door wet and cold. He still had a fever and was not feeling well. My mother got him to bed immediately and covered him with several blankets. She took care of him the best she could until the doctor arrived. The doctor said that he told her before that he would not make it in the Army. He said that he was sorry but my dad was not going to live probably through the night.

My mother was really upset at the Army for dismissing him this way. She thought that they could have at least given him a pass to fly home. We were so blessed to be able to see him before he passed away. We were surprised that he not only got through basic training but he had made it home.

My dad was actually blessed in a most horrible way. The ship, that my dad was on, took off from port a week later. It had on board, thousands of troops, including his fellow friends that he had gone through basic training. The horrific loss of life on the beaches of Normandy, France was probably on the mind of every soldier as they moved towards Europe. They were heading for Belgium where they would eventually be fighting, as I mentioned previously, in the Battle of the Bulge. Many did not return."

CHAPTER 19

<u>Polio</u>

.

CHAPTER 19

"After my dad got home from the Army, we started getting settled as a family. I was now two and one half years old. Our family was in the process of dealing with the Tuberculosis that my granddad contracted. The constant breathing in of sand in the Sand Hills was taking its toll on his lungs. When he got his store and properties sold, he made the move to Denver.

In those years, Denver was known as the Tuberculosis convalescent center of the nation due to the clear dry climate. There were several clinics where people would lie on beds in screened porches year around. It might be 20 degrees and they would be on those unheated porches.

We ended up with another medical problem. My sister who was six started complaining of her legs aching. My dad took her to a doctor and the doctor could not figure out the problem. He sent her home and told my dad to give her one half of an aspirin. Later in the week, I started complaining about the same thing. My parents knew something was going on and took both of us back to the doctor. The doctor had been doing some research since seeing my sister. He found that there had been an outbreak of Polio in the Denver area. He sent us to a specialist at Denver's Children Hospital where we were diagnosed as having Polio. Where we got this disease is still a mystery.

My sister and I were immediately taken to the hospital's quarantine ward. I had just turned three and was taken from my parents. They were not allowed to see us. This was devastating since I had just been reunited with my dad when he returned from the Army. Now I was taken from both of my parents.

Luckily, I was in a room with my sister. We had beds with tall vertical bars and rails so that we could not get out. It was like being locked up with prison bars. We were very active kids and now we were locked up twenty-four hours a day in a bed. There was no TV or videos in those days, no books, no games, no radio, and no visitors. They did not allow anything in the room because it might become infected with Poliomyelitis or what we called Polio.

A week later, my parents were able to get a doll into the hospital for my sister and a little toy monkey for me. This monkey became my best friend. I could pull a string and the monkey would crawl up a bar to the top of the bed.

I can remember one night when I was sleeping; the monkey fell out of the bed between the bars and onto the floor. The next morning a cleaning lady came into our room with a dust mop to clean the floor. I asked her to hand me the monkey and she ignored me and swept it away into the hallway. I can remember screaming and screaming as she swept it out.

My sister tried to reason with the lady but she would not listen. Maybe she did not understand our language. To her defense, she probably did not want to touch anything that might have the Polio germ on it. Being only three, I did not understand why I had been taken away from my parents and now they were taking away my pet monkey friend."

CHAPTER 20

<u>Freezing to Death</u>

CHAPTER 20

Well, the talking was keeping me awake, but Irv was snoring loudly. It was tough just lying there at the mercy of the elements knowing that we were both slowly freezing to death. Our strength had given up to the cold. We were praying that Jack had at least made it to the old mine shack. We both knew the odds were not in his favor to get any further. At least our friend would hopefully get out at daybreak without any health issues.

I lay in our snowy grave hoping that my wife had called the Colorado State Patrol to report that we were delayed getting back from Hall Valley. I was very concerned about my condition. I was getting delirious. I could tell that I was not in control of my thought processes. I was still shaking even though my body was getting numb all over. There was no escape and the thoughts of hope and courage were leaving me. I was having trouble mouthing words so I decided to shut up and give Irv a break. I kept poking Irv but he was not responding.

My competitive spirit was waging a war between living and dying. It was like a battle between good and evil. Why would God allow this? We were all born-again Christians. All three of us had families that were born-again and worshiped regularly at church with other born-again believers. Why would God turn his back on us when we were praying for his help? Why was everything that we tried a failure? Why didn't he answer the many prayers that we were sending to him? I was firm in believing that he was there listening. I kept thinking about the verse in Psalms that says, "In distress, I cried unto the Lord, and he heard me."

Then like someone hit me, my brain registered with a profound thought. He "heard me!" The God of the universe heard me! The heavens took a new meaning. The heavenly stars in the universe were beautiful as I gazed out from where we were lying.

It all came down to this. God was going to have to intercede if Irv and I were going to live. God was going to have to raise my dying and possibly dead body. My dead, hopeless, physical condition with my hands, my feet and legs, and my body, were in his hands because I knew that "He heard me!" This was comforting for my spirit although my body was still shaking.

This is all I had at this point. My body was dying. Even though help could arrive, mankind could not help with the deadness in my body. Only God could help. With the many hours frozen, now nine hours, it was hopeless as far as man could see it. God being with me made it mentally comforting in such an uncomfortable physical condition.

As the Psalmist said, "The Lord is my rock, my fortress, my deliverer, and my strength." "Whom should I fear." God was listening and working out his way of solving this problem. As a man, I could not see it. I just had to believe. This had to be faith. God said in Hebrews, "Faith is the assurance of things hoped for, the evidence of things not seen."

In all those years of playing baseball and basketball, I relied on my physical abilities to make me competitive. Now the Lord was battering me down flat on my back to show me that life was not about me. It was about Him. He put me prone on my back to worship Him and acknowledge Him. He was telling me that he was totally in control. This was when I relaxed and submitted to Him knowing that he would take care of the situation.

Some doubters would say that this is where I had given up all hope. If those doubters had Jesus in their heart, they would understand how God is in complete control of our lives.

My mind was still thinking in all directions. In between prayers, my mind would think back to all we had tried and failed. Even though I had told God that he was in control, I knew that he might lead me to another answer.

In my mind I knew that there had to be a way out. My mind wandered to a thought of being on the mound pitching. When I got tired and let batters get on base, I knew in my mind that if I were starting to fail, my teammates would pick up the slack. They were outstanding fielders and if I could just let a batter hit a ground ball or a lazy fly ball, I would be saved from ruin and the game would be won.

The competition was now the game of life. I was at the point where my skills on the mountain were failing just like being on the mound when tired. In this case, I needed to rely on someone else to get me out of this snowy predicament. God had a plan and he would provide a way. Maybe he would work his plan with someone, possibly my teammates, from the outside. Hopefully, someone, like my coach, would be walking to the mound of snow and asking me for the ball so that I can go to the warm showers.

Being a Christian, I kept thinking of scripture that the Lord had put into my mind over the years. This comforted me. My mind wandered to long ago in Egypt. The Hebrew people had hopes that Moses would lead them out of slavery. Being on this mountain buried in snow, I felt like I was in Egypt in slavery. There was no escape.

In Egypt, though, these hopes were dashed when Moses' good intentions led to worse conditions for them. Instead of gaining freedom, the people were worked even harder by the Egyptians who demanded that they produce the same amount of bricks with fewer resources.

This infuriated Moses. He cried out to the Lord, "Since I gave Pharaoh your message, he has only been more and more brutal to them, and you have not delivered them at all!"

I was in a terrible deadly circumstance that seemed to be going from bad to worse. My brain was moving back and forth sending me into depression and despair. But, just like in Moses' case, God always hears and answers our cries. His rescue plans sometimes don't kick in until all hope seems to be gone. The thing that was difficult in my mind is that God moves in His time, not ours. I told God that "I was ready when He was. And by the way, God, please hurry!"

My mind was remembering my wife now. I had been married only six months to a very attractive, intelligent girl. Man, I was proud to be seen with her! She was beautiful on the outside but also beautiful as a Christian on the inside. Was my wife going to lose her husband? Was her husband going to be crippled the rest of his life with no hands, legs, or feet? We hadn't even given thought of additional life insurance. I did have some that would at least pay for funeral costs.

My wife was an elementary teacher. All I could think was if I do get down the mountain; I would be crippled for life. She was such a beautiful woman. I did not want her to be lugging a multiple amputee around and supporting him the rest of her life. I knew that my feet had been frozen for hours and that life cannot exist in that condition.

CHAPTER 21

<u>Delirious</u>

CHAPTER 21

About 1:30 a.m., I was getting scared! I guess the weakness of facing death was finally taking its toll. I was unbelievably cold and my hands and feet had been frozen for 9 1/2 hours! I had no feeling in my limbs. Irv was sleeping and I was poking him at a regular rate trying without much success to keep him awake. My lips and face were frozen to the point of not allowing me to talk. My words were terribly slurred.

Earlier, Irv kept saying that he was getting warmer and he was not cold. I knew that he was getting close to freezing to death and his brain was telling him that he was warm. I was in constant prayer asking the Lord for help. This was the only comfort that helped. I was continually asking God for a miracle.

I looked up at the stars and then looked down at the sticks that I had laid in a neat "Boy Scout" pile for a fire. I had arranged them hoping that a spark from the snowmobile engine would ignite and make a nice fire.

Being rather delirious, I started pleading to God. "Lord, you told us in your word, 'For where two or three are gathered together in my name, there am I in the midst of them." "We are both Christians saved by faith and we have been praying to you throughout this night. Since you are right here, please at least light our fire."

I continued pleading, "Lord, I know that I don't need to remind you of your servant Elijah? He filled the trench around the Altar of Baal with water just to show the heathens that you were God. You sent your fire towards the altar and not only consumed the sacrifice, but also the wood, stones, and water!"

I have snow instead of water around my altar of sticks. Please send down your fire for us this morning?" Being delirious, I continued, "In fact, just a little spark will do. The stars are beautiful in this wonderful creation that you made. Maybe a falling star would come to the spot where my sticks are piled." I was remembering one of my favorite songs that Perry Como sang, "Catch a falling star and put it in your pocket . . . ." If I could just catch a small falling star and put it under the twigs for a bonfire!

I guess my mind was having a problem because I was "kidding" with a powerful God of whom I revere and respect greatly. I sure hoped that he had a sense of humor! I finally said, "I am sorry Lord. I am getting delirious and not thinking straight. I am only just kidding. I do not need Elijah's consuming fire, just a little spark." I was only about five feet from my sticks and I thought I might be in trouble if He sent that fire. We should have dug into the snow further off. I was thinking that when God does something, he does it in a big way.

It was getting harder and harder to keep Irv awake. He would just stir when I bumped him and he would go immediately back into a deep sleep. I looked up again at the starry sky and said. "Lord, I am not asking for much. Just a little spark to get this fire started." At that moment, I heard a faint buzzing sound. I looked up at the stars and thought that it was all over. I thought, "Lord, as requested, please, just a small spark."

Then it happened again and a thought flashed through my frozen mind! I jumped up out of the powder snow. Well, it was more like slowly moving out and slowly trying to stand. It took me a while because I was so stiff and clumsy. Being 6'10" tall, it probably looked like Frankenstein emerging out of the snow. I was so clumsy that I totally covered Irv's face with powder snow. This woke him.

It was hard with my frozen lips to mouth words since it had been a while since I talked to Irv. I tried to yell at Irv as loud as I could. I realized then how frozen my body was in and out. When I yelled, it came out like a hoarse whisper: "Sooommmeee one is coooommmming! Lithsssen!" I talked with such slurring words that I was sure that Irv did not understand. I repeated the words and pointed towards the bottom of the mountain.

Of course, Irv thought I was crazy. He knew we were freezing to death. The icy snow that I knocked on his face was working. He finally stood up but he did not look very pleased with me. He thought that I had gone totally off my rocker. We both stood still and listened. The breeze was blowing through the trees and it was difficult to hear anything. There was no sound. Did I just hear the wind? Was my mind going totally berserk? Here we were, about frozen to death and we were standing in a stiff breeze. Irv was giving me a look of astonishment that I did not want to see. Usually, when someone saw this look, they ran.

Indeed, I ran. I was sure that I heard something buzzing. Was God trying to do something for me or was he sending help. Maybe it was a snowmobile or some kind of rescue snow machine coming. As Irv watched with irritation, I scrambled to my snowmobile. It was a very slow procedure since I had been lying in the snow so long. My frozen ankles, knees, and hips felt like they were locked up. It was difficult with frozen hands but I pulled the starter rope and my machine started on the first pull. Usually it took several pulls? Was God looking out for us?

I started my machine because I knew the headlight would light up the area and show someone where we were. I pointed the snowmobile toward the direction of the buzzing sound. Hopefully, they would see the light. I decided that if I did falsely hear this sound then I would need to be a good actor so Irv would not do me harm. I did not want to say anything more to Irv for fear of what he might do. He was still standing in the same spot with a dazed, irritating look on his face.

I was about to collapse with an emotional trauma that was going through my body. So much hope and yet the wind was making me hear noises.

A few more minutes went by and I heard the sound again. I looked at Irv and he had a big grin on his face so I knew that it must be real. Then, we saw a light flashing about a mile off in the distance. Thank God! This was such an emotional high that it is impossible to describe. I was happy because freezing on the mountain was one thing but getting killed by my friend would not have been a pretty picture the next day.

Irv started moving quicker because he became a believer. I kept adjusting the direction of the snowmobile so the headlight would show our rescuer where we were stranded.

CHAPTER 22

<u>Footprints</u>

CHAPTER 22

After what seemed like an eternity, a person stopped his machine at the top of the hill and started hiking down the slope with his flashlight. I can't describe how this looked and felt. Irv and I went from dying on that mountain to living.

We found later that he was the caretaker of a tunnel system that sends water from western slope of Colorado to the eastern slope for the Denver water supply. Water flows through the tunnel under the Continental Divide from Dillon Reservoir to the east slope of Kenosha Pass. Dillon Reservoir is right in the middle of Ski Country Colorado where there is plenty of snow for water. It is surrounded by the Keystone, Arapahoe Basin, and Breckenridge ski areas.

I explained the best I could about the jam that we had gotten ourselves into. I was slurring my words so bad that he probably thought that I was drunk, even though I had never been a drinker. I had a terrible time mouthing words as if I was a stroke victim. It was exasperating that finally, after our hopeless wait, help arrived and I could not talk or communicate properly!

I explained the best I could, about the open pool and the impossibility of getting the machine through the broken ice. I explained the drive belt that I had broken trying to go up the slope to get around the ice. I showed him the new belt that we could not get on due to our cold hands.

He said that we needed to get out of there and he could take one of us at a time. But, it would be better if we could get my machine out so that we all could get out now. I was ashamed to tell him that we had spent hours trying to do this same thing.

He crawled up to his machine and brought back a crowbar. I could not believe how fast he made the trip back and forth. He had come down the trail that Jack had made up the hill. Irv and I had gone half way when we turned back.

It took both of us to work on the belt because of the hardness of the rubber due to the extreme cold. I held the belt in position and he pried with the bar. We tried about four times. Each time, I could not hold the belt right because of my numb hands. On the fifth try, the belt popped onto the pulley. A beautiful sight made more beautiful when I thought of all the wasted time I spent trying to get the belt on. I felt a little better seeing that a warm individual had problems with the cold belt.

We would have never gotten the belt on without the crowbar. He told us that he always kept this bar in his machine just for belts. This is where his experience showed. He had been at this sport many more years than us.

While we were working, we needed light to see what we were doing. I asked Irv to hold the man's flashlight. I had a terrible time communicating with Irv to hold the flashlight. He was in a different world. Finally, I took the flashlight and jammed it into Irv's stomach and yelled at him to hold it. You never did this type of thing to Irv if you valued your life. At this point, I didn't care. Thankfully, Irv got the point.

After we got the belt on, we needed to figure out how to get the machine around the ice hole. The ice was freezing but it was not solid enough to hold a 500-pound snowmobile as well as a 200-pound driver. He said that we would have to wade the pool.

I told the man that I was frozen from being in the water and I had no problem going into the water again to get the machine around the hole. Surely, I would not be frozen worse from doing this.

The man cleared out a trail as well as he could to the pool. He also cleared out a small area on the other side. He started the snowmobile and drove it to the pool. Irv and I were so extremely weak by this time that it was a good thing that this man was strong. He picked up the machine at the fight front. This was the engine end of the snowmobile and very heavy. Irv got on the right-back side of the snowmobile and I got in the middle on the left side.

They started walking on the right edge of the pool and I went into the water, breaking ice as I stumbled through. Although it was a struggle, we got it by the first water hole! The other holes were not that large. The man got on the machine and drove it by both. He continued on, driving the machine to the top of the hill. That was one of the most beautiful sights that I had ever seen! I was emotional. I thought that I would cry. Now I was worried about trying to walk up that hill. I had tried before with no success.

The man came back down the hill and I told him that we had tried to get up the hill but we were too weak. He told me to hang onto him and he would help me get to the top of the hill. It took some stumbling but he helped me up the hill. He did the same for Irv.

He asked me if I could drive my snowmobile. I told him yes. He said that he felt that Irv was not in a mental state to drive. He was right about Irv. He just stood there like he was in another world.

The man told Irv to ride double with him on his snowmobile and to grab on tight. Irv just stood there like had not understood one word. The man started his machine and pointed for Irv to get behind him. Irv finally realized what was going on and got on the back of the machine.

When we started going around the first curve, Irv fell off the machine. He either was so frozen that he did not have strength enough to hold onto the man or he could not think straight enough to hold tight. I was worried that he got hurt because I knew that there were rocks under the powder snow. He stood right up and walked to the machine and got on again. I heard the man telling him, "You have to hang on! Your life is in danger!"

The trip down the hill went pretty well from timberline. The man told me to follow him. I had trouble working the throttle with my right hand because it was numb. Because of this, I did not go as fast as normal because I was afraid of turning over my machine. They kept getting ahead of me and would have to slow down for me to catch up. I could make out trail going down as we went because of the tracks of someone who had walked there—my good friend, Jack.

It was now 2:00 a.m. pitch dark and sub-zero degrees frigid cold. My legs, feet, and hands had been frozen for ten hours. After what seemed like a terribly long drive, we saw lights ahead. A Colorado State Trooper was there with Jack and a friend, Bill who had driven up with his camper truck from Denver. Bill had his camper all heated up and ready for us.

The State Trooper told us to get going towards Denver because it would take an ambulance or helicopter another hour or more to get there. He asked if he should order a helicopter or ambulance. They could meet us at Bailey that was about 25 miles east. Jack told them no. He figured that we would have to wait for them to arrive. Precious minutes were being wasted. If we could get rolling, we could get to Denver soon.

The trooper offered to lead the way. I understand he drove in front of the camper with his emergency lights on to the hospital. Another trooper met us on the edge of the Denver metropolitan area and helped the other trooper escort us through the various signal lights. Bill and Jack said that they felt like VIP's.

When Jack thanked the man for coming up to get us, he looked a little puzzled. Jack had warned him that he should not follow all the snowmobile tracks since they went so many directions. He said that he had no trouble finding us because all he had to do was to follow the FOOTPRINTS IN THE SNOW. He was puzzled because the footprints took him directly to us! They never wavered off the trail that he knew so well!

CHAPTER 23

<u>Jack's Story</u>

CHAPTER 23

We got to the hospital in a Denver suburb, about 3:30 a.m. My wife had been called with the news that we were finally off the mountain. Jack's wife told her that we were going the hospital. She had been worried to death about her new husband. It had been one of those terrible days teaching the day before. She had two very wild, out of control fifth graders that just drove her crazy.

Totally exhausted, she fell asleep on the sofa. Later she told me that with praying, the Lord had given her a feeling of comfort. With all the terrible thoughts of whether I was alive or not, the Lord was with her! What a blessing it was to have a praying wife!

Later, in the hospital, I was looking through the Bible for passages that had the word snow in them.

I came across a passage in Proverbs 31:21: "She is not afraid of the snow for her household." Well, maybe my wife's sleeping was Biblical.

Jack had his own story after he left us on the mountain. He said that when he reached the top of the hill where he could look down where we were, he laid down in the snow for quite a while getting his breath and strength. He was wondering why he volunteered to go because his body and his mind were telling him that it was impossible. He had miles to go and realization came to him that he had a responsibility to us. This was a life or death circumstance.

He lay there and prayed to the Lord. He told the Lord that there was no way he could do this alone. He asked the Lord to intervene and help him to get down the mountain for his friends. He was so tired and weak and it was a struggle to stand up. He wearily stood there a moment and then slowly started walking. Every step seemed impossible. He would sink down three feet! He needed snowshoes.

He was in constant prayer asking for a miracle. After about a hundred yards, he began to realize that for every ten steps, he would have to pause, lay down on the snow, and rest. Then take ten more steps and lay down on the snow, and rest. This was demoralizing. He was so weak and his mind was giving up. His body just couldn't go on.

His mind was telling him to go back and be with us; walking out was impossible. The walking was getting more difficult in his weak state. Realizing the impossibility of the situation, Jack prayed to God for help to somehow reach the old mine shack.

All he could hope was that his wife had called someone for help. Maybe someone was coming now. He needed to get his mind clear so that if someone came to help, he could explain properly where we were.

He was stressed about leaving us and he was concerned about the shape that both of us were in. He knew the condition that I was in was grave and this kept him on his feet. He had to get down the mountain. How could he get energy to walk through this white jungle?

He realized that not only was he fighting deep snow but he was also fighting a brain that was telling him to quit. As he struggled through the deep snow, he began thinking about a song that he heard Bill and Gloria Gaither sing at a concert that we attended. The song was entitled, "Through it all." He started singing. "Through it all, through it all, I've learned to trust in Jesus, I've learned to trust in God."

Surely this God with whom he had a personal relationship could be trusted to get him down the mountain. Jack was telling himself that he just needed to trust in God, the deliverer.

The walking was not any easier. But at least his mind was clearing. If only he would have the energy to get back to the warm pickup and drive to Grant for help.

As Jack was walking and singing, his mind flashed back to remembering a book that he was currently reading. The author said that we should praise God in all situations no matter whether they are good or bad. God puts us in these situations to think about Him and to honor Him. The author was trying to say that it was these bad situations that we face that turned us to God for a deeper relationship. Good or bad, God has a reason for everything. Jack started praising God for this situation and that something good would come out of it.

His praise was not unnoticed. He slowly realized that the walking was now becoming easier. He continued looking into the heavens and praising God and thanking Him for the situation and thanking

Him for helping him through the snow. Jack realized in his praise, that he was not sinking deep into the snow! He was walking as if he had snowshoes on! This was impossible.

A critic might say that he was walking in the snowmobile tracks and the packed snow was what was making it easier. This might be true with the sun melting snow in the middle of the day. This was early in the dark morning with −20-degree temperature. The snow just doesn't pack down when it is all powder and this cold. Also, when we stopped our snowmobiles, we sank into the deep snow. We would have to power the machines up onto the top of the powder to move. There was deep powder snow beneath the tracks.

The Lord was listening to Jack's praises and was helping him. Even when he would see the track making a large sweep around curves, he would take small shortcuts through the snow. The walking was still easy on unbroken snow. This was deep powder! Irv had gotten stuck so many times on the way up in the deep powder. Jack said he could see where Irv turned his snowmobile around in the powder. Jack was able to walk right through all of this with ease.

He also was not feeling the cold as much now—probably because he was moving at a faster rate.

The skeptic would say that this was impossible. But when you look at the time it took Jack to go eight miles from where we were to the pickup, it wasn't much longer then an average hiker would take on the same trail in the middle of the summer. To walk through deep powder snow in this amount of time was humanly impossible. This was a miracle!

There was a problem that Jack had not contemplated. We were up here for the first time and did not know the country. We had investigated every nook and cranny. There were many mine roads and animal trails through the trees. Our snowmobile tracks were everywhere. It was dark and hard to see up ahead. He had to make countless decisions at a fork in the road to decide which trail to take. The trail that we took coming up was not necessarily a trail that was or going down on the way back. It was hilly mountain country so Jack could not rely on just taking the trail that was going down.

At every decision, he would praise and thank God for the situation and ask for the right direction. There was not one time that he had to stop and go back and retrace his steps due to a wrong decision! Every decision was correct! This is why the tunnel caretaker was puzzled. He followed Jack's tracks directly to us with no detours. He could not understand how someone not familiar with this country could walk directly out and not get sidelined.

There was one curve where the caretaker slipped off the trail due to rocks or timber underneath. When he got off his snowmobile to lift it back onto the trail, he could not understand something. The snow was so deep that he had a terrible time getting back up on the trail. But, for some reason, the footprints that he was following were on top of the snow. Praise the Lord!

From the caretaker's standpoint, this was virtually impossible. This was a human standpoint. With God, anything is possible! God had made the snow firmer and the direction clearer. Prayer does make a difference!

Jack was frozen and weak when he finally made it to the new pickup. It was closing in on midnight. He continued praising God. Now, he was trying to figure out how he would get us help at this late hour. Where was a phone? Would there be someone up at this hour that he could ask to use a phone?

He also had something else on his mind—heater. As Jack took out the key and fumbled with cold, frozen hands and fingers to unlock the door. He could not help but be thankful that he had made it to the truck that would be warm soon.

He put the key in the ignition and nothing happened! How could this be? What was he doing wrong? This was a brand new pickup. Was there something different about how to start it? The automatic transmission lever was in park so he tried starting it in neutral. Nothing! He had trouble finding the headlight switch because it was a new truck and he was unfamiliar with the dashboard. He turned on the headlight switch and nothing happened. He hit the horn and nothing worked. The battery was dead! This was a new pickup! He had just walked eight miles and the battery was dead! The light switch was off so what was it that ran the battery down?

Jack finally found the lever to unlock the hood. He thought that the battery cables might be corroded. He felt confused because why would the battery cables be corroded on a new pickup? It was so dark that he couldn't see. He found a flashlight in the glove box and looked at the cables. They seemed okay.

Jack found a wrench in the glove box. His hands were cold but he managed to use the wrench to loosen the terminal wires and scratched them for better electrical conduct and put them back on. Still nothing! It was looking as if the battery was completely drained of electricity and dead.

Time was wasting. This was so devastating that he felt delirious and totally frustrated. Every time he tried to do something, there was a dead end. He was shaking and freezing cold and he knew that we were in worse shape than him. He had to get help. As he closed up the truck, he began thinking about how God had delivered him down the mountain of deep snow.

He started running down the snowy road. Running was difficult with clumsy snowmobile boots but the road was snow packed where we had driven. It was sure easier then fighting powder snow. He needed to run about two miles to Highway 285.

Jack was in tremendous shape. He was the number one amateur singles tennis player in the State of Colorado. Normally, running was not a problem. But the lack of food was causing a problem with his stamina. He continued praising God and conversing with Him asking why Him why he did such a great miracle for him coming down the mountain? And yet, He seemed to be turning His back on him at the pickup. Finally, he made it to the highway with blisters on his heels from the loose snowmobile boots.

This early in the morning on this lonely stretch of highway, there was virtually no traffic. After waiting a while, a car came by. Using the flashlight, he tried to wave down the car but the driver did not want to pick up someone in the darkness. Who in his or her right mind would pick up someone in the dark with no broken down car in sight? After two trucks came by with the same success, Jack could not wait any longer.

He began walking toward Grant that was five miles east. He kept thinking that surely someone like a trucker with a CB radio would stop to help him. But it was too early in the morning. There were no other vehicles coming. He had to get going faster for help. He was sick with exhaustion. Even though he had no energy and had blisters, he started jogging awhile and then walking awhile, hoping to get to Grant as soon as possible. He decided that waving the flashlight and his arms was maybe causing a problem with the vehicles that had gone by. He started putting his thumb up when a vehicle would come around the corner but still no takers.

Jack began to seriously think that he would not make it. His energy was totally spent. He continued praying and praising God. He sat down at the side of the road and prayed some more that someone would stop. He told God that he had come to the end of all energy and needed help.

He did not see any lights from vehicles so he started walking again. Thank God, he got to a straight stretch of highway and he could see lights from the town of Grant some distance away. This was a small town with a few buildings. It looked as if there were two or three streetlights in front of the buildings.

He had a burst of adrenaline hit him when he saw lights and the dream of a warm place. He was worried that no one would be awake. A thought came to him about the townspeople. How would they react to a person who looked half frozen and frosted over? Would they react just like the cars that would not stop for him? Would anyone answer a knock at the door? He started praying that someone would be there to help him.

When he got to Grant, there were lights on at the local bar and some pickups were parked outside. Thank God someone was there. Inside, there were about five locals and a bartender. He was surprised that this many people hung out that late or maybe early. He figured that it was because it was a weekend.

It was so nice going into the door into the warm room. Inside there were two men sitting at a table and two men sitting at the bar talking with the bartender. Jack said hello and said that he had a serious problem above Hall Valley. Could they help him? He explained how the two of us were stranded at timberland. No one showed any interest to help! They just turned away and continued drinking and talking to each other. They didn't want to be bothered!

Jack was completely dissatisfied with their non-caring attitude. He had walked 15 miles in the middle of the night in sub-zero temperatures and was not going to let this happen. He repeated the problem and asked what was wrong with them. He told me that these were big men. They all out weighted him by 100 pounds. After what he had gone through, he was at the point that he did not care what they did to him. There were two lives at stake and he was not going to give up now. One man replied to Jack that none of them had snowmobiles and then turned away.

Jack looked at the bartender and asked him if he knew anyone who could help or at least let him use his phone to call the Colorado State Patrol. The bartender stood there a moment and then said he was welcome to the phone. Then a thought came to him and he told Jack about a tunnel caretaker who lived west who had a snowmobile. The bartender called the caretaker and explained the problem. In about a half-hour, the man was at the bar and talking to Jack. He said that he would be glad to help.

Jack apologized to him about how early in the morning it was. The man said that he was an early riser and this was not a problem. Jack asked him if he knew where Webster Pass was and the man said "Like the back of my hand. I go snowmobiling up there every weekend. I have not gone in the last couple of weeks because the powder is too deep." Jack explained how we got up there and how we were coming down. He explained the sharp turn on the road at timberline. The man told him he knew about where the curve in the road was and he would get up there as soon as possible. Jack told him in a kidding way to not forget to take matches.

While waiting for the caretaker to come to the bar, Jack called the Colorado State Patrol and explained the situation. A state trooper was on his way to Grant to survey the situation. Jack told the caretaker that he would stay at the bar and come up with the trooper. Jack also had called our friend Bill in Denver asking him to bring up his camper and his two snowmobiles in case they were needed.

Jack called his wife to tell her about the problem and that he was okay. He told her that we were in serious trouble and he did not know if we were living or not and to pray for our deliverance. His wife was put in the terrible position to call the other two wives. Our three wives had called each other and had talked about getting help. They were not sure what to do. When she called my wife, she said that Jack had called and had told her that the "boys were in serious trouble."

CHAPTER 24

<u>Peel Socks</u>

CHAPTER 24

When I got into the camper, our friend Bill had it heated and had hot tea and soup waiting. He tried to help me get my boots off. My boots were frozen to my socks and my socks were frozen to my skin. He took a knife and cut the boots in pieces, peeling the boot from the sock. Finally, all I had was socks frozen to my skin. It was impossible to get them off. Bill and Jack decided to get my snowmobile suit off and cover me with blankets since I was shaking uncontrollably. The socks would have to come off later. Precious time was wasting getting me to a hospital.

They stopped in the town of Conifer about 26 miles east. The State Trooper asked if he should order an ambulance to wait on the outskirts of Denver. Bill figured that it would just take more time for me to be transferred to an ambulance. He told that patrol that I needed hospital attention. All an ambulance could do was get me warm and I was getting warmed up in the camper. Why transfer me through the cold into an ambulance. It would take too much time. He figured that he would just drive to the hospital. It should be a fast drive with no cars on the road in the early hours of the morning.

Jack took over driving and Bill got into the camper to work on my socks. I worked my way down to the table area where Bill could help me. The socks were still attached to my skin and Bill worked and worked to peel them off using his pocketknife.

My legs from my knees down to my socks were paper white in color and were totally numb. Bill was afraid to cut the rest of my socks off for fear that my toes might come off with the sock. Bill was able to cut and peel my socks down to above my ankles. He decided to wait on the rest and let the hospital personnel do the rest. He was afraid of doing more damage. I was still shaking uncontrollably now and he knew that I needed to get to the hospital as soon as possible. I had the shakes since 4:00 p.m. the previous day.

I got back into the bunk above the pickup cab and covered up with blankets. I thanked Bill for all he was doing. It was so nice being in his warm camper. At least, the bunk was at the top of the camper where it was the warmest. I shook for the next hour as we drove towards Denver.

I could tell they were making good time by the way the vehicle was swaying on each curve. At last, we made it to the hospital. The ER personnel were waiting with a gurney to take me into the emergency room. They worked very fast to help me get my clothes off to determine what damage had been done. They told me that I was experiencing frostbite. Duh! They told me to be patient; a doctor would examine me further.

CHAPTER 25

<u>Frostbite</u>

CHAPTER 25

Frostbite is the opposite extreme of a burn or scald. A burn or scald will destroy tissue. The same is true at the opposite end of the spectrum with frostbite. The freezing cold stops the circulation of the blood. It is like someone putting a tourniquet on your arm for several hours. The blood flow is stopped. The arm will die after a short time if the flow of blood is not there.

In the case of frostbite, if the tissue is not attended to and warmed up, the cells will be permanently damaged with possible death to the affected tissue. The frostbitten part of the body affected becomes very white, hard, cold, and numb. The numbness is very noticeable. This is basically the start of death to the portion of body affected. You might say; a tourniquet has been applied. Later as the tissue thaws, it becomes red and extremely painful of which I can personally tell you.

If there has been little blood in the part before this death, the gangrene is dry; if normally filled with fluid, moist gangrene results. Gangrene is dead flesh. It turns the tissue to a black color and the underlying tissue and bone are dead. It is extremely painful as the flesh dies. Bacteria do not commonly infect dry gangrene. The results usually mean that the limb will become shriveled and mummified.

The opposite is true with moist gangrene. It has an offensive watery discharge and becomes infected increasing the chance of complications. Amputation of the part is usually necessary to save the person's life because gangrene spreads rapidly through the bloodstream. Every effort must be made to prevent the dying tissue from becoming infected. The bottom line is: any long-standing blockage of the flow of blood through a region will cause its death. The object is to get the blood flowing through the tissue again before it becomes gangrenous.

Simply, if the tissue is not thawed out, it dies. If the tissue is totally frozen, then gangrene will be present when the tissue thaws and the limb will have to be removed or the patient will die. I was glad that I did not know all of this before I went into the hospital.

CHAPTER 26

Emergency Room

CHAPTER 26

It seemed like an eternity for them to get me out of the camper and into the hospital emergency room. A doctor on call finally looked at me. He agreed that I had frostbite and needed immediate attention. It was now about 4:00 a.m. I lay for about an hour alone and naked on a cold, hard table in the cool emergency room before they took me upstairs. I thought the doctor told me that I needed immediate attention. I had known for hours that I needed immediate attention. I did not know how they defined "immediate."

During the time I was in the ER, they would not let my friends in to see me. They said that immediate family only was permitted. I told the nurses that they had saved my life and therefore, they were my immediate family. The nurses would not listen. I was still cold, numb all over, and still shaking uncontrollably. My feet were still frozen. The camper had helped with the warmth but it had not thawed them out. I was in misery. The hard table was terribly hard and cold. I thought that they had put me naked on a morgue table instead of a hospital table realizing that I would not live long.

The emergency room got real quiet when I was lying on the table. The ER people left, maybe for a coffee break. I was alone and still freezing and had been told nothing. I was concerned and not happy about how I was frozen and shaking uncontrollably and I was left an hour with only a towel over my waist area. No one even came to me to ask what they could do to make me more comfortable. I thought that they could at least offer me a blanket.

Were they waiting for another doctor? Were they waiting because they felt that I was a goner? Had my wife, who I had just married six months ago, been contacted? Were they waiting for her to arrive? I needed blankets! Many of them! I needed to be thawed out. What further damage was happening because of this wait? Would this extra time leaving me frozen cause complications and possibly death? I had read that if you have frostbite, you should get the

240

limb warmed as soon as possible to keep from having dire consequences.

Finally, two ladies dressed in white came in and took me upstairs on the elevator. They gave me a blanket to wrap myself in for the trip. The two nurses helped me into a large tub of water that was about 100 degrees.

These two nice looking nurses helped me into the tub. I was totally stripped and a little shy but when you are shaking uncontrollably and in pain, you get to the point where you don't care. I just needed to get warm somehow. Just get me into the warm water and get me taken care of. They were monitoring the water temperature to keep it between 100 and 105 degrees in the tub. One nurse sat with me the hour or so that I was there. She kept adding more hot water to keep it at the proper temperature level.

I was looking so forward to this hot bath! Now that I was in the water, it was one of the most painful experiences that I had ever gone through. It was worse than sprained ankles like I had in basketball. These were pretty bad.

If you ever had icy cold hands and put them into warm water to thaw them out then you would know what I was experiencing. The pain is excruciating. In this case, my arms, hands, legs, and feet were frozen. It was one of the most painful experiences in my lifetime. It was torturous! I was not sure that I could take more. I thought that I might pass out with the pain but I didn't care. My mind was telling me to get out of the tub because of the extreme pain. I told them that I couldn't take it and to let me get out.

I tried to get up but the nurse would not let me. She yelled out for the other nurse who came in for support. I eyed both of them to see if I could take them. I was too weak. If I had been in there alone, I would have gotten out. The one nurse told me that the doctor ordered this and if I wanted any chance of saving my hands and feet, I should stay in the water. Again, I thought that I would pass out with the pain. Up on the mountain, I dreamed of getting into a hot tub but now the dream was a nightmare.

After about an hour of torture in the tub, my shakes finally started subsiding. My thinking now shifted to a worry about dying of pneumonia.
I heard later that in some cases people died because as several body parts thaw out, the extreme icy-cold blood starts to circulate into the heart causing shock.

The heart just stops. This, I found out, was another reason why the nurse stayed with me the whole time.

The two nurses finally lifted me out of the tub into a wheel chair. This was tough because I had no strength in my numb legs. Also, the strength was not there in my arms and hands. I could not use them to leverage myself to get out of the tub and into the chair. Here I was a big tough athlete and I could not even get out of a bathtub. Being as tall as I was, 6'10," did not help. My height made it tough on the nurses. They were not used to someone as tall as I was. They had trouble getting under my arms to gain leverage. My armpits were taller then they were.

They were trying to be careful not to touch any part of my limbs and were very careful getting me into the wheel chair. They told me not to touch anything with my hands, legs, or feet.

As they wheeled me down the hallway to a room, my thoughts were that I should get used to the wheelchair. If I didn't die from this condition, I would probably be in one of these wheel chairs the rest of my life.

They put me into a bed with a special foot frame designed to keep anything from touching my feet. My two legs and feet were still mainly pure white. Some blotches of pink were showing in the upper parts of my legs. They told me not to touch the frostbitten skin if possible. It might ruin the tissue that was frozen. This is why they built a frame. The sheets or blankets could not touch the skin.

They spent about an hour trying to get the frame adjusted. The problem they were having was that they had never had someone 6'10" in one of these beds that were designed for someone with a maximum height of 6'2". They finally got a maintenance man to take the footboard off the end of the bed so that I could hang my feet over the bed. He went down to his shop and came back with a sheet of plywood that he slipped under the mattress to extend the bed.

The nurses brought handfuls of blankets and built the end of the bed up to the mattress height. When I saw all the blankets, I asked that they put them on top of me but it didn't work. After they got the extension figured out, I asked for five blankets. Finally, two and one-half hours after getting to the hospital, I got the blankets I needed.

I told them that I had not eaten for 36 hours and I was terribly weak. One nurse went out and came back with juice and crackers.

As my feet and hands thawed out in the tub, the intense pain started. It was a constant, vicious throbbing pain. I was told that I had experienced frostbite so deep and severe that it probably should have been called deep tissue freezing. I understood later that gangrene was usually waiting in the deep tissue.

It hurt me to touch anything with my feet, legs, or hands. I could not handle anything because my fingers were so painful. Even trying to pull the blankets up or push them down was painful. Dialing the phone to talk to my wife was a problem. I could not dial the rotary phone. My wife brought me a pencil to hold in my hand to dial. I could bypass my useless fingers using the pencil. Such a small thing made a huge difference!

CHAPTER 27

<u>Visitors and Pain</u>

CHAPTER 27

Sleeping was a problem with the pain. They gave me medication for sleep, but sleep was hard to come by due to the constant pain. I did not care what they did just so they did something because I was so demoralized with the pain. It reminded me of being on the mountain when I was trying to start a fire with gasoline. I was so cold that I did not care if something had blown up. Up there with hypothermia setting in, I was thinking that I would enjoy a forest fire.

One day a chaplain came into my room to see if he could do anything for me. I could tell that someone had given him a negative report in the hospital about my situation by the way he talked. I told him that I was doing great. I quoted him a scripture from Philippians, "For me to live is Christ and to die is gain."

I don't know what type of chaplain he was, but he felt very uncomfortable and speechless. He did not know what to say so he left. Most chaplains that I had seen would come to a person's room and ask if they could pray with them. This chaplain just left. I felt sorry for him and prayed for him. I never saw him again after that.

I was in the hospital for fifteen days and over 100 people came to visit me. That was probably why I ended up in a room at the end of the hall where visiting people would not bother others. They were such an uplifting element to my dilemma. Talking with them kept me upbeat. Visitors averaged around seven each day. I wish that it was only seven but on weekends the number might be 15 all at once. I was blessed to have so many friends and relatives concerned about me!

Jack, Bill, and I were teachers at a Denver suburb high school of about 1,800 students and 120 teachers. Everyone was concerned. I lost track of the vast number of get well cards that arrived. I am sure that the hospital was getting tired of all the people and cards. I cannot remember how many telephone calls came in to that room. The good part is that it kept me busy. It took my mind off amputation.

There was a tremendous thing that happened through this tragedy. These guests, Christian and non-Christian, heard the story of God's love and miracles on top of the mountain. If it weren't for Jack's miracle, we would not have made it off the mountain. I showed them the impossible in our sight and showed them the proof of the possible through our Christ Jesus and his miracles. I told the story over and over. Praise God!

One thing that would happen is that people would come in the door and sometimes come toward the bed to shake hands with me. I would have to say that my hands were too sore to shake hands.

I tried not to show the guests my frostbitten hands and toes unless they asked. I would warn them that the sight was not pretty. This was one of the most hideous sights that I have ever seen. I know that my wife had trouble looking. I could tell it in her eyes. She was kind of squeamish about a lot of things but I know that it was tough to see her husband this way.

When I would show the visitors, most of them turned away because they could not stomach the sight of my blistered toes. They had trouble looking at my nine red fingers and my right small finger that was twice the normal size due to a huge blister that formed. It was a not a good sight.

I could tell by the look on their faces and the glancing eyes toward each other, that they were sure that I would lose everything. After seeing this, I could see that they did not know what to say. They didn't want to say the wrong thing. They did not know how to act seeing someone in this condition. I tried to ease them by saying something comical.

Before I showed them my hands and feet, I tried to tell them that it looked terrible but I still had all my toes and fingers and this is a plus. After I showed them my hands and feet, I told them that I was a living miracle. God had performed miracle after miracle to get us off the mountain. Why would I give up on God now? He would perform a miracle and heal me.

I would tell of Jesus' burial and his new body. I explained that I buried my dead body on the mountain and through the love of Jesus; I would soon have new hands and feet. I would tell them that someday, I would be walking normally again. I could see in their faces that they were thinking that I was beyond another miracle. Many of them were born again Christians and I knew they were praying for me but the terrible sight even discouraged many of them.

My heart would break thinking of my beautiful six-month bride having to go through this mess. She was a 5'10" tall, slender, black haired beauty. She had beautiful white skin. Her black hair and high cheekbones came from a great grandmother who was part Cherokee Indian. I was so proud to be with my wife because anywhere we went people would admire her beauty. Now I was worried that someday, she might want to turn her back on an ugly, maimed husband in a wheelchair.

She was a trooper! She was so supportive during my whole ordeal. I never saw her with a negative view. She was always upbeat and happy as she would enter the room even though I knew she had a tough day in her classroom. I cannot explain how wonderful it was when she walked into the room. It was as if a bright light came on.

I would watch the clock in the afternoon and would always look forward to her getting off work teaching and coming to visit me. It was so uplifting to me due to the stress of the medical situation. She would always come into the room smiling and showing her love. She became my most positive influence in my earthly life. When I would feel a little down, my whole outlook would change with her support.

No one has experienced a true marriage until they have a Christian wife who prays and puts all of your trials and tribulations into her Lord's hands. I firmly believe that without my wife's support and prayers, I would not be writing this today.

I should not have survived on the mountain let alone this time in the hospital. My mind was constantly focused on survival. I was facing possible blood clots, likely gangrene, and amputation. Black coloring was starting to show on my toes. I would ask the doctor about the blackness but he would be evasive. This made me feel as if serious complications were on the rise unless the grace of God intervened.

I would ask the doctor every day how my feet and hands looked. I always got the same answer, "We have to give it some time." The doctors really did not know what direction this would turn. All they could do was give me the proper medication and rest and do the waiting game.

I was living moment by moment in time instead of day by day. Every moment was one of the most painful and stressful moments in my life. I knew in my mind that when the doctor was saying, "We have to give it some time," he was saying we would take off the dead parts when the time is right.

My prayers were constant. My wife, family and friends were constant prayer warriors. Our minister was praying. We attended a large church in Denver. Many of the members were praying. At the church, my name was on the 24-hour prayer chain. This meant that every hour, someone was praying for me.

Even my parents' church and my sister's church were praying. My wife contacted her very large family in Texas. She had close to one hundred cousins. All of her relatives and members of their churches were praying.

I had an army of Christian Saints praying for me. Angels had to be surrounding me. If Satan and his demons even tried to get close, they were bombarded by the power of prayer by these loving Christians. The Christian family is not one to mess with.

These people had held me up in the presence of our Lord and Savior, Jesus Christ. This is the same Person who is running our universe. I felt honored that all of these people, by the hundreds, were praying for me and that God would intervene. From a human standpoint, the healing of my frostbitten fingers and feet seemed hopeless. I had been frozen too long. Long freezing means gangrene or death. From a heavenly standpoint, anything is possible with God. God raised the dead!

I can remember being always upbeat with very little depression. Of course, I had stress and some depression. I was human. There was a pretty good reason to be terribly depressed if I would let my mind dwell on the situation. Knowing that I was probably going to face amputation did, of course, cause stress beyond anyone's imagination especially when I was alone. Being in constant pain did not let me think about anything except my condition.

I was fortunate that so many people were concerned about me. People who I did not know were praying every day and keeping me in His loving arms. I was so thankful by how I got this far physically and mentally. I was constantly praying and thanking God for his deliverance.

It was a strain, though, on my new marriage. I wanted, in a big way, to be alone with my beautiful wife. Every time this started to happen, either some people would walk in or a nurse would come in with medication. These were the days when hospitals had visiting hours. By the time my wife got off work and to the hospital that was across town, other people would be getting off work and arriving. Some visitors would still be there until 9:00 p.m. when visiting hours would be over. We had a couple of very nice nurses who felt sorry for us when they found out that we were newlyweds. They would let my wife stay a little after visiting hours was over. This was special!

I was sure that facing the unknown was almost too much for my wife to handle. I would feel so sorry for her when she left. I wanted to go with her and comfort her! She was my new wife. I was supposed to take care of her. After she left I would lie in bed with tears in my eyes and pray. I would feel so lonely. I would look so forward to my wife coming to visit and now she was gone. Everything negative thing about my dying body would come to the surface. The enemy was attacking me. I would continue praying and sleep would finally come.

Because the God of salvation was with me at this terrible juncture in my life, I would go to sleep knowing that he cared for me and would take care of my wife. I stood on his promises. He promised that my wife and I were sheltered in His arms.   His scripture says in Romans 8:28, "And we know that all things work together for good to them that love God." I surrendered everything to Him.

CHAPTER 28

<u>Stomach Shots</u>

CHAPTER 28

I still have bad memories of my two-a-day stomach shots. One thing that bothered me at that time was that I would get this shot from a four-inch long needle going into the center of my stomach at about 9:00 each morning. It was really something wonderful to look forward to.

I understood that they were giving me a blood anticoagulant to get the blood flowing and help to keep me from getting blood clots. About an hour after the first shot, another person would come into the room and give me another shot, right into the middle of my stomach. This was not fun.

After four days of this, I casually asked the second person why I was getting two shots so close to each other. Why not get one in the morning and then the other in the afternoon to spread them out. He looked rather disturbed and looked sheepishly at me and said that he would check. The next day, I just got one shot.

When the doctor came in about ten that morning, I asked him why I got only one shot. He said the hospital had mistakenly made two punch cards with my name on them for medication and I was really only supposed to have one punch card. I was getting double shots and double medication. Maybe all the double shots and double medicine was why I was feeling chipper most of the time.

When you are in a hospital, you are at their mercy. By faith, you assume that they know what they are doing. Sometimes it can be fatal. When the doctor told me about the mistake, I asked if there would be a problem. Of course, he said no. Here I got down the mountain in one piece and had gone through all of this pain and now was I going to face a problem with incorrect medication? I prayed for several days after that asking the Lord that no harm was done.

I was continuing to have problems with my special uncomfortable bed. I was having trouble sleeping because the bed just did not fit me because of my extreme height. I was spending 24-hours a day in that bed and this was getting old. The bottom was falling apart at least once a day and sometimes in the middle of the night. The blankets would shift around and fall off.

The nurse strapped sponge rubber pads around my ankles and heels to protect them from the sheets or blankets. After a few days, I was allowed to walk into the bathroom with assistance. They would not allow me to walk on the front of my foot with my toes. I had to walk on my heels on these pads. It was wonderful just to get out of bed.

The worse thing of all was when the surgeon would come into the room every morning to check how I was doing. He would tell me that everything was going fine so far. He tried to be honest with me. He had told me after his initial examination that it was impossible to be frozen as long as I was and "not have serious consequences." He would not tell me what those consequences were but I pretty well knew.

I was sure that our family doctor was talking to my wife in private. In my mind, I was imagining the terrible things that he was probably telling her about my condition. I was frozen too long. Something was going to have to come off. I never asked her about this.

Our doctor was a frostbite specialist. The hospital called him when frostbite victims came in from the ski areas. He initially told me that it was a waiting game. Every day there had to be an inspection to see if gangrene was present and then do whatever was appropriate.

I wasn't sure that I wanted to know the real truth. It bothered me when I knew that the doctor was probably talking to my wife in the hall.

The surgeon, of course, would not mention gangrene. I could tell what he was poking around for with his scalpel. He would carefully inspect every finger and toe. Of course, why would a surgeon be examining me every morning for fourteen days? He had a reason. The time would come. He was just waiting for the right time.

Every day I was in severe pain physically and severe pain mentally. I was in a waiting pattern to be wheeled down to surgery. I was just waiting for a day to come where surgery personnel would be coming into my room with their surgery table.

Every time I heard someone rolling a cart or some noise in the hallway, and this was many times a day, my heart would start beating fast. I could feel the blood running up into my face. It was terribly hard to always have a raging battle going on with the uncertain. The unknown of all of this was always my enemy. It was constantly on my mind.

The fear of the unknown time reminded me of when I was so small and WWII was going on. They took my dad away and my mother left soon after to join him in California. Also, when I was three, I was taken away from my parents because of Polio. Shortly after that, my mother was wheeled down the hospital hall because she had appendicitis. In my young three-year old mind, I was losing her, again. Here I was a small boy who was in a constant battle with the unknown. The same feelings were going through my mind twenty-seven years later and it was not something that I could control.

CHAPTER 29

<u>Black Feet</u>

CHAPTER 29

A doctor who specializes in frostbite at a Denver hospital talked with me one day. He was a doctor that many of Colorado's frostbitten skiers went to for treatment.

He told me that in my case, my frostbitten limbs were pretty well lost after about five hours in the sub-zero weather. I had broken through the ice at 4:00 p.m. My feet and legs started having tremendous pain and started going numb soon afterwards. My boots and socks were saturated with water and they were frozen solid.

I was not "thawed out" in the hospital bathtub until approximately 6:00 a.m. This was 14 hours that my limbs were frozen! This doctor told me that by all means, my feet had died and possibly my hands. This is why the surgeon came in every morning.

Day by day for fifteen days, I waited for the surgery. My view from the window at the hospital was a brick wall. This was a typical hospital building that had been added to many times. Every time my dad visited, he would ask if I had counted the bricks yet. I tried many times, knowing that my dad would be back, but it would get to a point where my eyes would seem cross eyed because there were so many bricks. I would have to start over.

After 10 days, my toes and right finger were looking worse and worse. Slowly, the blisters dried up or broke and were replaced by a terrible black crusted covering. I got to the point that when someone visited; I would put my right hand under the sheet so that they did not see it. All of my toes looked as if someone had torched and burnt them. They were all very black. When someone asked to see them, I usually refused to show them at that time.

When I showed someone, I could see in his or her eyes that the rumor mill had been working. My friends and relatives were all thinking that that surgeon would soon be doing his work. Of course, many of them had talked to my wife who told them that it was critical and to pray.

It was hard for me to watch the surgeon do the examination. He would take out a scalpel and probe in the black mess to see if he could see any dangerous problems. After the tenth day, he became more concerned with my right small finger. When he came in, this is where he would look first.

On the morning of the fifteenth day, the surgeon came into the room and examined me as usual. I was worried because he had my family doctor with him. My family doctor had never been in the room with the surgeon before.

He turned to my family doctor and said, "I don't understand what has happened with this young man, but I think he is out of the woods and can go home." I almost fainted. I was so emotional and my eyes were tearing up that I could not talk. God was in control and was making a statement. What happened was medically impossible. My doctor concurred that only a higher being could have possibly done this. I thanked them both and also thanked my heavenly Father.

Leaving the hospital that afternoon with my wife and looking at the sky and everything else was about the most wonderful feeling I have ever had. It was right up there to when I heard the buzzing sound at timberline. As the days progressed, the terrible black looking flesh on my finger and toes started to crack open. It took several weeks but day by day, the black peeled off to beautiful natural baby skin. I still have my legs, feet, toes, and fingers! I write this story on a keyboard with normal usage of my fingers, even my right small finger.

Most people who have had frostbite complain about going outside in the cold air. Their limbs tingle and bother them. I do not have any of these conditions. Cold does not bother my limbs. In fact, I still live in cool, colorful, Colorado. The winters are cold but the cold air does not affect my hands or feet.

CHAPTER 30

<u>To God be the Glory</u>

CHAPTER 30

I am grateful for my friend, Jack, who walked thirteen miles through deep snow and impossible odds to find help for me. He saved my life. There are countless other people that I appreciate who helped and inspired me. My teaching friend, Bill, drove his warm camper to meet me when I came down the mountain. He brought soup, hot chocolate, and thankfully, blankets! My hunting and fishing partner, Irv, spent the night buried with me on the cold, frozen mountain for seven hours. He is probably still in shock over having to lay there listening to my life story. I appreciate him very much. Also, I thank many great church friends and family who prayed for me in my terrible condition. Of course, I am grateful for my loving, beautiful wife of six months who never gave up hope. She was my constant friend and prayer warrior. Most of all, I am grateful for my wonderful friend, Jesus, who never left my side.

Jesus died, was buried, and rose again with a new body on the hill called Calvary. With my experience, I had to bury myself frozen on a hill called Webster Pass. I had determined that my life was over. Parts of my body were dead and I figured that the rest of me would surely follow. Miraculously, with the blackness I was experiencing, I was renewed with a new body by the power of the Holy Spirit. The doctors could not explain it. Having Jesus in my life made the difference. Jesus answered prayers and changed my life.

At times, people fall into life's cold freezing holes. They dig and dig trying to climb out of this hole hoping that life will be improved. They just sink deeper and deeper and get hopelessly colder and colder. Their minds get frozen and muddled and they see everything in discouraging ways. Sometimes their bodies are in situations that are hopeless.

On the East side of Webster Pass, I buried myself in a cold grave of powder snow. For my hands and legs to last that many hours in sub-zero temperatures was humanly impossible. Yet God prevailed! Only God could have helped me off that hill. God guided Jack in a miraculous way in a straight line down that mountain, leaving <u>Footprints in the Snow</u>. My rescuer, who came up the mountain to rescue me, followed those same footprints. Those footprints, blessed by God, led him directly to me. My rescuer was an experienced mountain man who knew the area like the back of his hand. He was astonished that someone like Jack, who did not know the mountain pass very well, was able to walk straight out! He also did not understand how someone could walk out in 3-4 feet of powder snow without snowshoes. Thank you Jesus! Only you could have done this!

I am reminded of the poem "Footprints in the Sand." When Jack came down that mountain, he was walking side-by-side with our Lord and Savior and yet there was only one set of footprints in the snow.

God provided Jack the way for my rescue! It is hard to imagine that God in his glory in the vast universe would take time to take care of me. But, I know that He loved me because I was his child. A father takes care of his child.

Only God could have taken someone like me, who was buried in a frozen tomb, and give him a new body. There is no other answer from the doubters or critics. This was a hopeless situation—a medical miracle.

Your situation might be just as bad or worse. But just think—Praise the Lord Jesus that this situation might bring glory to His name. Ask the Lord to deliver you out of this abyss. Ask him to show you how this terrible situation, that you are in, might be a blessing to others.

The reason might be to help you bring a loved one to Christ or a friend to Christ. Thank your loving God that you are in a position that might help lead this person to Him. You are now in a position to witness to someone by physically showing him/her how wonderful it is to have Christ in your life!

Remember the Apostle Paul with his thorn? He said in II Corinthians, ". . . there was given me a thorn in my flesh, to torment me, but, My grace is sufficient for you, for My power is made perfect in weakness." (NIV) Thank God that you have become stronger because of this thorn in your side.

Your thorn might not be a large thorn like I had. It might be a very small thorn. Treat it the same way. Thank the heavenly father that this situation might be used for Him. Remember that God is the creator of the entire universe. He sees things in the large realm. He uses our small problems to make us aware of the big picture.

In conclusion, everyone at some time in their life will run into a dead end in their job, an impossible medical issue, a broken marriage, or some other problem that to them there is no way out. They feel hopelessly buried. I pray that they will read this miraculous story and realize that anything is possible with God, even when buried in an impossible situation.

Continually pray and believe that "The Lord is my Rock, my fortress, my deliverer, and my strength. Whom should I fear?" Read God's word! He will deliver you through your difficulties! Receive Jesus into your life today! He will help you through these cold freezing holes!

ꛠꛠꛠꛠꛠ

14999962R00155

Made in the USA
Lexington, KY
04 May 2012